Skill, Strength **Agility, are all in**
requisites of a R
Player but there is...

"No Substitute for Pace"

Ray Hewson

Published in 2024 by Ray Hewson

Copyright ©Ray Hewson 2024

ISBN: 978-1-0686599-0-4

Cover and Book interior Design by Russell Holden
www.pixeltweakspublications.com

This work originates from the author's own records plus research, combined with information provided by individuals whose contributions are gratefully acknowledged elsewhere in the book.

Photographs are not always of the best quality.

Dates are given where reasonably confident of accuracy. Where actual dates are unknown, the general period has been used.

This book is dedicated to:-

Colin Hewson - BA Sports Management Northumbria University:

Chief Executive South Lakeland Leisure 2002-2006:

Principal Consultant Tribe Intelligent Culture Change from 2008 who has edited the book and constructively aided it in a variety of ways.

Acknowledgements

Front Cover photo:- (supplied to me by "Gentleman Jim" Lewthwaite in 1996)
"Gentleman Jim" racing in for another try against
Western Districts at Orange in N.S.W. on the 1946 Tour.
Rear Cover photo:- (supplied to me by Frank Castle in 1996)
Thanks to local author and friend Stan Henderson for his regular advice.

To Russell Holden of Pixel Tweaks Publications for his valued assistance.

I must also pay tribute to exceptional sources of information I have used to research and confirm my own records:-

Alex Service and Saints Heritage Society.

Colin Booth who was once regarded as "The busiest boxer in the British Army" and who was of splendid assistance in regard to Bruce Ryan.

Margaret Cazabon , Parliamentary Web Manager Department of Parliamentary Services ,Parliament House, Canberra ACT 2600.

Melinda Andrews of Athletics South Australia.

Steve Hewett of The Centre For Sports Science and History at Birmingham University for his instant response to my request for help in establishing detailed results of all sprint events in the Barcelona Olympic Games and information on the 1990 Commonwealth Games.

My thanks are due to A League of Gentlemen – not all of whom are with us today, but all in past decades , displayed above average interest in my work and made considerable effort to help out in the supply of photographs and other valuable information:-

Arthur Bassett, David Bolton, Frank Carlton, Frank Castle, Arthur H. Daniels, Les DyI, Willie Horne, Jim Lewthwaite, Ralph McCarten, Mike Murray, Ike Southward, Jeff Stevenson, John Stopford, Mike Sullivan, "Drew" Turnbull, David Watkins.

Apart from the eminent authors whose work I have used to research and confirm my own records and who are listed at the end of this book under the heading Bibliography, I pay tribute to the late Brian Miller without whose eye catching illustrations the book would have been just that much less interesting to the reader.

Definitions: -

Even Time is the clocking of 10 seconds, by a sprinter, for a run of 100 yards , or 10.94 seconds for a run of 100 metres. Hence the oft used description of such athletes "Even Timer".

Inside: on occasion used to describe a performance when the athlete clocks a time better than 10 seconds for 100 yards or 10.94 seconds for 100 metres.

Scratch: defines the starting mark of the runner in a handicap race who must complete the full distance as opposed to others in the race who receive starts. For example, in a 100 metres handicap race the "scratch" runner would run 100 metres whilst giving advantageous starts to others in the race. There are occasions where there is a "Virtual Scratch" runner in a race i.e. he/she may, in the 100 metres race described above, be starting off say 2 metres thus running 98 metres but still having to run further than all of the other competitors.

Back Marker: the athlete in a race where he or she starts from the least advantageous handicap mark or possibly even from "scratch" i.e., giving a start to all the other competitors.

CONTENTS

INTRODUCTION

Carrying the ball and in football gear on the field of play are my provisos necessary for the title "fastest".

There are many players who have reputations for exceptional pace. How realistic those reputations are is debatable in many cases. Take for example the small player who, generally, is able to move his arms and legs at an alarming rate and, consequently, gives the impression of great speed. But is he so very fast ? Let's face it,some are but some are not. But, over the years this game has existed there has probably been a preponderance of fast athletes not equalled in any other sport, except of course in track athletics itself. Some of those, from bygone eras, who fit this category I have recorded in this work.

"Although speed is an essential ingredient of success for wingers, centres and half-backs, it is an advantage for all players to be fast. Speed takes the ball carrier into and through a gap in the defence. It enables the support player to be in position, and a player to follow and gather a kick; it helps the ball carrier to run round the opposition. When defending, speed prevents a player from being vulnerable. There are more players who have not fulfilled their potential because of a lack of speed than for any other reason, so it is common sense for all players whatever their position to increase their running speed."

(The Rugby League Coaching Manual by Phil Larder. National Director of Coaching 1988. Published by Heinemann Kingswood.)

What Phil Larder said in 1988 is still valid today. For the purposes of this book, I have generally used the word "Pace" instead of "Speed".

I am also reminded of comments made by Ray French,in 2014, in regard to the pace of an England R.U. winger of the early 1960s:-

"....John Young, who I had the pleasure of playing alongside for England. He was a genuine sprinter and only required a slight overlap down the touchline to race past any defender. He might have lacked a sidestep to beat his opponent, but a swerve and blistering pace would see him past all but the very quickest of wingers."

Ray also recalled the pace of:- *former European Games 100 metres sprinter, Berwyn Jones, sprinting down the wing for Wakefield Trinity and coasting around myself and a couple of other St Helens' defenders for a try at Knowsley Road. Barrow's former wing flyer, Mike Murray and Leigh's Rodney Tickle, two supreme sprinters And two of the greatest wingers of all time in both codes of rugby, former Commonwealth Games athlete and St Helens record try scorer, South Africa's Tom Van Vollenhoven, and the legendary Aussie, Brian Bevan, who starred for Warrington………. I must confess to him still racing past Saints' international second row flyer, Dick Huddart, and myself for a try at the corner for Blackpool when he was aged 42 years! An outstanding professional sprinter too on the Northern tracks in the Forties and Fifties." (July 2014)*

One of my aims with this work is to give readers the opportunity to widen their knowledge of many of the past "heroes" of the game of Rugby League viewed from the angle of pace, as well as acknowledging some of the athletes that play the modern game.

Having taken up sprinting some 75 years ago, simultaneously with my first interest in Rugby League watching the Barrow team of the late 1940s, it wasn't long before I became aware of pace men such as Jim Lewthwaite, Brian Bevan, Cec Mountford et al. From then on I was hooked for life with this obsession regarding such players and who was the fastest. Certainly in that post war period through to the 1970s at least, sprinting times were often difficult to obtain because of a great interest in professional running by Rugby League players who didn't wish to disclose performances because of a possible knowledge gain by opposing competitors and also the handicapper would have an open eye and a listening ear for any information that could wrongly be advantageous to sprinters in the handicap races prevalent in the professional athletics scene. Misleading information was often all that was available and reputations either inflated or deflated. Such practices have existed for as long as I have been following the game and been involved with sprinters. The secrecy and the often misleading information adds to the glamour surrounding players' abilities. It has always been difficult to acquire "the goods" on any particular athlete, particularly in the world of the professional sprinter, which has always had a good sprinkling of League players. The assumed name, the training session in out of the way scenarios, the training clothing perhaps including a balaclava hat so that recognition was difficult if not impossible, all formed a part of the rugby league/professional sprinter's world. Such traditions are not entirely dead, even today. I have been able to quote times for the players covered in this book and I have been able to check such performances and request the reader to note, to the best of my knowledge, they are on record bona fide achievements. Many of the players mentioned in this work, I have seen. Others, of course, played even before my time. Those I have witnessed are indicated in the text by surname in capital letters. I hope that in the following pages I convince the reader that pace cannot be replaced. It's importance in achieving success in rugby of both codes cannot be overstated and there is

"No Substitute for Pace"

ADAIR Bill: (1930 -)

(Many thanks are due to Alex Service and Saints Heritage Society who supported my research into Bill Adair including Bill's photograph.)

Bill Adair was a late starter to Rugby League who had originally, at the age of 18, displayed his prowess as a sprinter in The British Army.

On leaving the service in 1950, aged 20, he was persuaded to sign for St Helens and found himself making his debut on the left wing against the touring French club team "Canaries" of Carcassonne on 5th October 1950 at Knowsley Road with the onlooking circa 16000 spectators. After two years at Knowsley Road Bill went to Liverpool City the club that had started out as Liverpool Stanley. Eventually he had trials with Warrington and one game with Leigh but it is his time with Liverpool City that I have concentrated on in regard to Bill Adair's pace.

The spotlight fell on this arguably little known winger in the 1953-54 season when his club, Liverpool City, who were bottom of the Rugby League - one division only in those days - faced up to a mighty Warrington side who were in fact top of the League. This was the season that the great Brian Bevan became the highest try scorer in the game's history held up to then by Saints Alf Ellaby. Even though City were at home and the crowd was swollen with Wire fans who had travelled the short distance between the two clubs, the result was a foregone conclusion and it was a case of just how many points would Warrington pile up and how many tries would their great wingers Brian Bevan and Stan McCormick score. **Bill Adair faced up to the great Bevan. The result of the match was one of the shocks of the decade - City 5 Warrington 2 - but more importantly, as far as this work is concerned, the game supplied the opportunity for Bill Adair to emerge from his relative obscurity. He is certainly remembered for his efforts that day of chasing and catching the Aussie wizard all over the field. The speed required to achieve such a feat was, to say the least, considerable and from that day on Bill Adair was a much more respected winger noted for his excellent turn of pace.**

ALBERT Darren: (1976-)
"Just Another Saints Flyer"

This undoubted speed merchant, between 1996 and 2006, played for Newcastle Knights, then Cronulla Sharks in his homeland Australia before signing for St Helens in England's Super League competition from where he eventually returned to play again for Cronulla. There have been many very fast athletes who have played the game and many of them have been subject to diverse opinions as to whether they could actually play Rugby League. I am pretty sure Darren Albert did not fall into this category. Scoring in excess of 70% of the games he played verifies that.

In 1999, Darren was unofficially crowned the fastest man in the Australian NRL after winning a race on The Footy Show, running 10.7 seconds for the 100 metres. Whilst he was at Knowsley Road with Saints in 2004 he became "The Fastest Man In Super League". The title became the property of the popular Aussie after a competition at Robin Park in Wigan where, in full rugby gear and carrying a rugby league ball, he finished first in a seemingly effortless 100 metres sprint on grass, clocking 11.37 seconds. The event was a sell out with fans unable to get into the ground. The winner also collected £2,000 for his efforts.

Darren had arrived at the English Super League in 2002, but a few years before that his sprinting abilities had been well and truly recognised by Australian pundits and trainers. It was recorded that he could perform in the mid 10 second range over 100 metres at virtually any time and without specific training. It wouldn't surprise me if The Saints Flyer clocked around 10.5 seconds either. Opinions were aired that he could have represented Australia as a sprinter had he decided to take that course of development in his sporting career. His technique as a runner was highly praised, a testament to which I can add my own opinions in that he looked the part on the rugby field - he ran in the classic mould of a top sprinter.

Darren Albert was the true version of a rugby player who could certainly have made a great track sprinter.

(Many thanks are due to Alex Service & Bernard Platt - Saints Heritage Society who supported my research into Darren Albert.)

ANDERSON Jock: (1919 - 2003)
The Powderhall Flyer

Huddersfield is a club that found a taste for Scottish R.U. players and one raid over the borders about the time of the Second World War produced a flying winger. **John "Jock" Anderson was a well-known sprinter who had competed prominently in the Powderhall Handicap, the New Year's Day annual contest that brought the best professional fliers to Scotland from all over the world. During that period "Jock" was a very big name, a Scottish Rugby Union international winger who had featured against the All Blacks in Scotland's defeat at Murrayfield on 27th November 1935.**

After signing from Hawick Rugby Union Club, the flyer won ten medals in his seven years at Fartown, scoring 74 tries in 114 games.

The Powderhall Flyer
(www.huddersfieldrlheritage.co.uk)

ASHTON Eric: (1935 – 2008)

The tall athletic frame of Great Britain Captain Eric Ashton pictured in June 1962 as Great Britain play Australia in the First Rugby League Test at Sydney Cricket Ground. (GB 31 – AUS 12). Dave Bolton also pictured with Kangaroo great Ken Irvine and, on the ground looking up, Billy Boston.

(Photo gratefully acknowledged and permitted for publication in 2012 by Mitchell Library, State Library of NSW. [d7_12645].)

A contender for the title Greatest Centre Three-quarter Ever, this rangy and exceptionally classy athlete of Wigan fame in the '50s and '60s formed a terrific partnership with the powerful Billy Boston. You don't score 300+ tries in a Rugby League career unless you can run! Ashton achieved this feat and my own abiding memory of this great centre is to see him some 50 to 60 yards out from the opposition line, Boston on his right hand and a defence waiting for the pass to the mighty Welshman. The pass never came on many occasions, for Ashton would see hesitancy in the defence and race away down the touchline, his long legs eating up ground, to score without a hand being laid upon him. For me. Ashton was an awe - inspiring sight, so athletic, so balanced, so powerful and further testimony to his pace was his performance on the 1958 tour when he scored 30 tries, only surpassed by Mick Sullivan. This was a touring team that had considerable pace in the form of Frank Carlton, Jim Challinor, Bill Wookey, Ike Southward, Mick Sullivan, Alex Murphy and Dave Bolton.

In the following paragraphs I have extracted from the excellent item by Dennis Whittle in the St Helens Star 26 March 2008 who pointed out that the legendary Great Britain Test Captain was the first player to be honoured by the Queen. Born in St Helens Eric Ashton spent his entire playing career at Wigan. Beginning as a winger he became a prince among centres and one of the most decorated icons in the game's history. Standing 6ft 2ins and tipping the scale at 14 stone in his heyday, Eric Ashton was a centre cast in classical mould, being blessed with pace, handling skills, an uncanny ability to read a game and excellent leadership qualities. Whilst at Rivington Road School the talented young athlete was a Town and Lancashire County choice at schoolboy level and trained with Saints B team but, remarkably in view of his later achievements, was not offered professional terms by the Knowsley Road board. Whilst on National Service in the Royal Artillery the Central Park rivals signed him after he starred in a Rugby Union game at Murrayfield in 1955. The future renowned centre went on to play 497 games for Wigan, scoring 231 tries and kicking 448 goals before retirement in 1969. **Ashton's scoring feats and pace are put even more into perspective and reflect the fact that he was a Services double sprint champion during his National Service days.**

Eric forged a lethal right-wing partnership with fellow legend, Billy Boston, that is etched indelibly into Rugby League folklore. Certainly a gentleman of the game he was sent off just once, against Leeds in 1961, following a difference of opinion with fearsome "Farmer" Jack Fairbank, who also got the early-bath treatment. Eric skippered Wigan in a record six Wembley finals including against Saints in 1961 and 1966 when he was awarded the MBE and had his best-selling life-story, **Glory in the Centre Spot**, published. Following coaching appointments with Wigan then at Leeds he returned to St Helens in 1974 and accepted the coach's job at Knowsley Road. Silverware was soon on Saints' sideboard, with the Championship lifted in 1975, while the Challenge Cup, Premiership and Floodlit Trophies were all won during the next season. A Premiership encore arrived in 1977, followed by Wembley defeat versus Leeds 12 months later, prior to Eric handing the coaching reins to Kel Coslett in 1979-80. An invitation to join Saints' board came in 1982 and Eric, who supported the team in boyhood, became a much-respected ambassador both for the club and Rugby League in general. He occupied the hot seat of Club Chairman from 1993-1997, twice leading out the side in the Wembley conquests of Bradford, thus becoming **the only man to captain, coach and be chairman of Challenge Cup-winning teams.** He was also at the helm when the inaugural Super League title was lifted in 1996. **Eric earned 26 test caps - 15 as captain - between 1957 and 1963. He was a member of the Ashes-winning squads in Australia in 1958 and 1962, the latter as the first skipper St Helens born. He also figured in the Great Britain World Cup party of 1957 and was skipper of the winning 1960 squad. He was honoured with life membership of the Rugby Football League and presidency of Saints and was bestowed with the code's ultimate Hall of Fame accolade in 2005.**

On the great centre's passing in March 2008 former Wigan and Great Britain teammate, Billy Boston summed the feelings of many when he said: *"Great player, centre and gentleman, what more can one say about Eric Ashton? He began as a winger but it was a lucky day for me, Wigan and Great Britain when Ash' moved into the centre spot."*

ATKINSON John "Atky": (1946 – 2017)

This Roundhay Rugby Union Club flying machine signed for Leeds RLFC in May 1965 and appeared for the first team on debut some 10 months later against York scoring two tries. **Between 1966 and 1982 "Atky" registered 340 tries in 518 games for Leeds then, between 1982 and 1983, 4 tries in 20 appearances for Carlisle, the team he went on to coach for a couple of seasons. This superb left winger had a colourful representative career with Yorkshire-15 appearances and 10 tries; England – 15 appearances and 11 tries; Great Britain Tests and Tour games – 26 and 24 games - 12 tries and 24 tries respectively. A career totalling a staggering 618 games and equally impressive 401 tries. Not many can pride themselves on playing in 4 World Cup series – he did in 1968, '70, '72 and '75.**

Seven Yorkshire Cup Final victories between 1968 and 1980 were part of his curriculum vitae against Castleford, Featherstone Rovers, Dewsbury, Wakefield Trinity, Hull K.R. (twice) and Halifax. **With a great Leeds team 1968, 1977 and 1978 Challenge Cup Final triumphs came his way** at Wembley against Wakefield Trinity, Widnes (after the best part of a year out with a broken leg and wrist) and St Helens. **The 1970 BBC2 Floodlit Trophy and the Players No.6 Trophy** in 1973 fell to Leeds with Atkinson facing St Helens and Salford. **League Championships** didn't escape this great winger's portfolio of victories either, with victories over Castleford in 1969 and St Helens in 1972. **Inducted into Leeds and The Rugby Football League Halls of Fame**, here was a winger who, like all Leeds outside backs, was respected whenever he played. Perhaps underrated in an era when "the greats" were going "over the hill", John "Atky" Atkinson scored many tries that less pacy wingers could not have attempted. **Given the ball he was always a dangerous thorn in the side of any opposition. Tall and weighing in around the 13 stone mark, during his career, he was the fastest man on the Leeds payroll and, it could be reasonably argued, the fastest winger in the game. A hair raising sight when in full flight – a most extraordinary athlete.**

BATTEN Eric: (1914-1993)

Eric Batten in top gear at Toowoomba,- Saturday 13th July 1946, scoring one of his two tries for England against "The Downsmen".

Eric Batten was a fine athlete of strong physique who, even though he possessed great pace, knew that the best way to the line was in a straight run during which he had been known to "hurdle" over opponents just like his father Billy had done before him. Eric certainly knew his way to the line and displayed, even at the end of his career, pace that in his youth

The National Library of Australia's assistance in obtaining the image of Eric Batten is gratefully acknowledged. Reference-: [No title (1946, July 14). Truth (Brisbane, Qld. : 1900 - 1954), p. 7. Retrieved July 3, 2023, from www.nla.gov.au/nla.news-article203128299.]

must have caught many defences lacking. This is borne out by the fact that it is reported that Eric was winning pro sprint races both before and after the Second World War. I was fortunate enough to see Eric, play for Featherstone Rovers. He played Rugby Union for Sandal (West Yorkshire) before signing for his first club in Rugby League in 1933 – Wakefield Trinity which commenced a playing career lasting over two decades in the game that saw him play for Trinity again in the early 1940s, also for Hunslet scoring 194 tries, Leeds, Castleford, Bradford Northern, Featherstone Rovers in the late 1930s,early 1940s, mid-1940s and early 1950s. Representing Bradford Northern 233 times, Eric touched down 165 tries. For Featherstone Rovers he scored 62 tries over 105 appearances including as a guest in 4 games. His appearances for Wakefield, Featherstone, Leeds, and Castleford between 1939 and 1945 were as a World War II guest. This unique winger also represented England on 13 occasions scoring 6 tries, Great Britain on 4 occasions registering 1 try and also a Rugby League X111 against a Northern Command X111 (A regional Command of The British Army) in 1942. **In 1946 the Australian press reported on Eric as** *"England's most dangerous winger"* **and** *" England's hurdling wing thee-quarter".*

Eric appeared in eight Challenge Cup finals, five for Bradford Northern, two for Leeds, and one for Featherstone Rovers. **In all of his career appearances he registered a massive 443 tries bettered only by Brian Bevan, Billy Boston, Martin Offiah and Alf Ellaby.** He coached at club level for Featherstone Rovers, and Batley and is a Featherstone Rovers Hall of Fame inductee.

BEVAN Brian: (1924 – 1991)

Very special thanks to the late Brian Miller, without whose occasional eye-catching illustrations this book would have been just that much less interesting to the reader.

A brilliant resumé **"Bald, toothless chain smoker who staggered Rugby League"** by the late **Frank Keating**, Monday 20 November 2000 in **The Guardian** is referred to below in italics through this item on Brian Bevan. Frank Keating was the Guardian sports pages' prime columnist for more than four decades.

Bevan's Try Scoring History

The Bondi Streak played for Warrington, Blackpool Borough, Representative appearances including Other Nationalities.

For Warrington he made 620 appearances and registered 740 tries;

for The Seasiders 42 appearances and 17 tries;

in 26 Representative games 39 tries.

An unmatchable total of 796 tries between 1945 and 1964.

The greatest attacking wing three quarter the game of Rugby League has known. Don't let anyone fool you into thinking anything other than just that. On the field of play looking toothless and bald, padded up with protection that was yet to be invented commercially, this frail, almost comic looking, man was the biggest draw in the game in the late '40s and '50s, also the biggest scourge of defences. Given the ball almost anywhere on the field he was just as liable to score as not. An Australian who escaped, he played all his senior football in England. **"The Bondi Streak" remains unique 80 years on.**

Frank Keating recalls:- *"Bevan was born in 1924 at Sydney's Bondi. His father had played for Eastern Suburbs but the boy, though keen enough and fast, showed scant aptitude for the game's hurly-burly. At 18, the World at war, he was drafted as a stoker on the cruiser Australia. In 1945 she fetched up in Plymouth for a refit.*

On shore leave, the 21-year-old caught a train to Leeds and asked for a trial. Headingley was totally unimpressed by the skinny tyro, ditto Hunslet two days later. He tried Warrington and, because a family friend back home, Bill Shankland, had once played for the Wires, they gave the boy an A-team run out. The following week he was in the first team and signed up for £300 on the promise that he would return for a season after sailing home to be demobbed. True to his word, he was in his place on the wing at Wilderspool for the start of the 1946-47 season - and he ended it with 48 tries, 14 more than anyone else. The legend was up and running. And how."

Bevan set try scoring records that will never be matched. During several seasons he scored more than 50 tries and in 4 seasons 60 plus, with one season, 1952-53, a total of 72 tries. It wasn't just luck that made the inimitable "Bev" as good as he was, but years of practice from Bondi Beach as a child through the great years at Warrington and finally to Blackpool Borough where he played for a short time. Practice and training that had been greatly influenced by his father. Bevan had an approach to the game that in today's heavily hyped-up scene would even have seemed scientific; he apparently left nothing to chance.

My abiding memories of this fine athlete are of an occasion at Barrow's Craven Park when he scored past the Barrow fullback after a 25 yards run and a sidestep that was performed so close to the Barrow player that he truly must have believed he had Bevan in his grasp, when, in fact, he was totally unable to lay even a hand on the great wizard of wing play. Another occasion was Wembley in 1954, the dour Warrington - Halifax drawn final, when late in the game Bev fielded a kick just behind his own line and set off to beat virtually all the opposition in a tremendous run, the style of which you would not believe had you not seen him produce similar efforts throughout his career. With only the Halifax full back Tyssul Griffiths to beat, Bev, of whom it was said, "If there's only the full back to beat, then there's no one to beat", decided to pass to the supporting Bob Ryan who knocked on with the line at his mercy.

Keating continues:- *"Before, and since, a host of Australian rugby superstars have played and settled in the north of England. But none more superduper than Bevan. He remains probably the most vividly astonishing, and unlikely, man ever to lace a boot of either rugby code.*

Even in my sheltered 1950s west country boyhood, news seeped down of this phenomenon who could jink like a crazed pinball and run like a barmy hare and who weekly for winter after winter thrillingly injected with adrenalin the north's sporting culture and self-esteem."

Frank interviewed such as, for instance, Bev's also famed compatriot **Arthur Clues**, who shared many a pre-match hotel room with Bevan:-

"At any code of rugby there's never been a better than Brian, nor ever will be. Mind you, for a superstar athlete there's never been one less athletic: bald as a coot, no tooth in his head, a skeleton in braces. We'd be in twin beds. Every time the alarm went off before dawn I'd poke

out my hand in the dark to turn it off, and every time I'd find his false teeth chomping at my hand from the bedside table... that would be Brian's signal to light up, and for the next two hours he'd lie there on his back chain smoking, fag sticking up like a periscope, cough, splutter, cough, splutter. Then he'd finally rouse himself - to spend hours bandaging his knees - before going out that afternoon to make utter, bamboozled fools of some of the greatest rugby league players there's ever been."

Robert Gate the game's greatest historian wrote "The Great Bev" in 2002 a long-overdue biography of Bevan and recalled he was just old enough to see him in action once - in 1964, the winger's final first-class appearance under the spectacular moorland pelmet at Halifax's evocative Thrum Hall ground:-

"He was 39 and like forked lightning, he was absolutely, staggeringly brilliant. I remember spectators all around simply couldn't believe what they were seeing. And he hadn't just been doing that for a season or two but week in, week out for 19 seasons. I treasure a film of Wembley in 1950 with Bev haring and jinking all over the arena so you think, 'This film's been speeded up' - but then you look at the background and every other player is moving at ordinary, everyday speed."

Another of the game's vivid historians, **Geoffrey Moorhouse, was first awestruck at Wilderspool in 1947 by a length-of-the-field Bevan special,** *"a spindle-shanked fantasy"* against Wigan: *"Bevan was actually in-goal at the corner-flag when Gerry Helme desperately slung him the ball... at once those heavily bandaged shanks began to revolve, the tongue came purposefully out of the sucked-in cheeks and the toothless gums.*

This bald-headed wreck of a man's first shimmying sidestep or two takes him past the first three Wigan players before he was off, swerving across the field to beat two more, before straightening out and, by what devices I couldn't see, crossing at the far corner before any more defenders could catch up with him. He had run much further than the length of the field, he had swept from one end of it to the other in a diagonal; and he had gone through the entire Wigan team in doing so."

Frank Keating further comments:- *Bevan died in 1991. They packed Wilderspool for a memorial service and Colin Welland dignified the honours with heroic commemoration.*

"If a similar skinny eccentric turned up there asking for a trial 55 Novembers on, I daresay they wouldn't even let him near the pitch.' **As Robert Gate puts it sadly:** *"They'd say, 'Clear off, lad, go away and put on four stone and then come back and we'll see if you can run into somebody'."*

[Author's Note: Colin Welland was a lifelong rugby league fan who supported the game in newspaper columns and stood up for Rugby League against Rugby Union discrimination in the 1980s and 1990s. He won the Academy Award for Best Original Screenplay – Chariots of Fire.]

Extracts from a letter I wrote to Robert are worth recalling here:-

"Dear Robert,......................

Spike Hughes who played for London Irish and Austria once said, (and I paraphrase loosely,) :- **'The Author will be considered to have understated preposterously by those who know what he is talking about and to have exaggerated beyond the bounds of decency by those who don't.'** He was commenting of course on Michael Green's hilarious book "The Art Of Coarse Rugby". I feel the comments could equally apply to your own magnificent effort in " The Great Bev ". ....
"experts", will never be able to appreciate such a player as Bevan, never mind believe he was as good as he was, so your book will at least,hopefully, make them aware that there used to be a game called Rugby League and that such great exponents of the art did in fact play. Those of us who were privileged to witness the great winger's performances know that there is no exaggeration whatsoever. The one thing that actually hit me..........
was just how consistent he was. I mean, I knew it all the time, but to see his career laid out in front of one, as you have so ably achieved in the book is quite mind blowing. I saw some great performances from Bevan, but these Warrington fans saw it week in and week out. That was not fair! The significant comments by various of your contributors on Bevan's style, one of which by the late Tom Mitchell which mentioned his musculature brought back the view of my own that Bevan was certainly not lacking in leg (thigh) musculature, and it was very probably this that created the power for his lighting speed.

Thoughts on his crowd pulling power. At Barrow it was always "Is Willie Horne playing this week "? that was on most peoples' lips, except when Warrington were the visitors when it was "Is Bevan playing ....?" **Yes, there is much more one could say about the greatest attacking winger of all time, and he was indeed worthy of a book in its own right. Robert Gate's "The Great Bev" (2002).**

Let it suffice to say that all of the feats performed by Bevan were fueled by several basic factors - great overall speed; amazing acceleration; deceptive change of pace; a sidestep par excellence; all borne out by performances such as a 9.6 seconds 100 yards (10.5 for metres); his 100 yards in 9.9 seconds in full football gear at the Festival of Britain Sports in 1951,equivalent to 10.8 seconds for 100 metres; and a win over British Professional Sprint Champion W. Spence of BIyth, in a handicap race. Note: Spence (Real name Albert Grant) had actually run almost 11 yards inside even time when winning a Pro race in Australia over 126 and three-quarter yards in 11.6 seconds in 1950. When rugby league instituted its Hall of Fame in 1988, Bevan was one of the first on the list to be inducted and eventually was the only player to be inducted into both the English and Australian Halls of Fame.

BLISS Johnny: (1922 - 1974)
"Blistering" Johnny Bliss - "The Man From Chinchilla"

Photograph by kind permission of the family of the late Johnny Bliss,

Geoff Day at Penn Sport and The Manly-Warringah Sea Eagles (2012).

Chinchilla, "The Melon Capital of Australia", is 185 miles northwest of Brisbane in Queensland, Australia. The Annual Melon Festival is one of many events all of which have some, rather loose in some cases, relationship to the fruit. The small town of Chinchilla was barely 45 years old itself when a certain John Charles Bliss was born into its community on 30th August 1922. Johnny Bliss was destined to become a distinguished athlete. By the time he was 17, as a member of the Sydney suburb North Narrabeen Surf Lifesaving Club (NSW) over 600 miles(1000km) away from his birthplace, he was beginning to embark on the Beach Sprinting part of his sporting life that would become unsurpassed in its standards of achievement.

Before I venture any further in this item on Johnny Bliss, I must acknowledge the assistance I was given by the late and great athlete's wife Mrs. Joan Bliss. The lengths to which she went on my behalf are deeply appreciated.

The Beach Sprint takes place, not on a synthetic track or grass but, as the title implies, on the sands. Lanes are allocated to the runners,of which there may be up to ten, and the race can be anything between 70 to 90 metres. Competitions take place at all levels, from club to national and even international standards.

Johnny Bliss was exceptionally fast, so fast that between 1939 and 1953 he took out the individual Championship on no less than seven occasions at State and National levels. Additionally, between 1952 and 1971 he was a member of Championship winning

relay teams on no less than nine occasions at the same levels of competition. He also represented New South Wales State teams. Arguably the greatest beach sprinter ever, the legend's beach sprinting history is worth recording here:-

New South Wales State Beach Sprinting Individual Championship:-

Winner in 1941, 1944, 1947.

New South Wales State Beach Sprinting Relay Championship:-

Winner in 1960, 1963, 1965, 1966, 1971.

Second in 1961, 1967.

Third in 1962

Australian National Beach Sprinting Individual Championship:-

Winner in 1946, 1947, 1952, 1953.

Second in 1949.

Third in 1939.

Australian National Beach Sprinting Relay Championship:-

Winner in 1953,1959,1963,1964. Then 1971 as Coach.

Second in 1952,1962, 1965, 1967.

Third in 1954,1960, 1966.

Fourth in 1961.

"Blistering" was unquestionably an appropriate nickname for one who possessed such natural speed of foot. The North Narrabeen Surf Lifesaving Club honours the memory of Johnny Bliss by presenting to successful members in championships - The John Bliss Medal awarded to the Club's most successful competitor in the championship carnivals at Branch, State and Australian levels and there is also a John Bliss Team Award. The medals presented to the winners by Mrs. Joan Bliss annually. Joan told me about Johnny's great comedic talent and the lengths he would go to in order to raise funds for his causes, both in the Surf Lifesaving and Rugby League scenarios. Johnny was a skilled ballroom dancer and an excellent mimic. In **"The Sea Eagle Has Landed"** - The story of the Manly-Warringah Rugby League Club – there is even an item under the heading **'"Blistering" Johnny Bliss — Fastest Joker Alive'.** In relation to Johnny's activities after he had finished competing on the beach and playing Rugby League, Joan said **"I might also mention after his retirement from competing he continued training at our oval nearby, coaching many runners and footballers including the great Bobby Fulton when he came to play for Manly. He was contracted by Manly-Warringah as speed-running coach."**

As a young man aged 16, simultaneously with his Beach Sprinting, Johnny was playing junior Rugby League for The North Narrabeen Surf Club, originally as a hooker, but before long, his pace being acknowledged, he was switched to the wing position. Eventually at first grade level in Australia's New South Wales Rugby Football League "Blistering" Johnny Bliss would represent Balmain Tiger, North Sydney Bears (where he certainly became a cult figure) and Manly-Warringah Sea Eagles – the former between 1942 and 1943, then 1944 to 1946 and 1947 to 1953 with the latter two clubs. With the northern suburb district of Sydney club, Manly-Warringah Sea Eagles, he actually played in that organisation's first ever game at the top level of Rugby League in Australia. Topping the try scoring lists for his clubs almost became regular, with this happening at North Sydney Bears and at Manly – Warringah Sea Eagles.

Representative football first came his way in 1945 and between then and 1951 he represented City against Country on four occasions. This is the annual game that takes place between a side that represents municipal Sydney (City) and the rest of New South Wales (Country). City were victorious in all of those fixtures with Johnny Bliss scoring three tries. **On just one occasion, June 11th, 1951, Johnny Bliss played for Australia, in the First Test against France, at Sydney Cricket Ground, which the Kangaroos lost 26 points to 15.**

Ken "Arko" Arthurson, legendary player, coach and widely honoured administrator of Australian Rugby League knew "Blistering" Johnny well as a player at Manly-Warringah and ventured the opinion that:-

".......he could run like a deer. And Blissy had fast feet. I don't think I've ever seen a player who could get into top gear so quickly. He would go from zero to 100 miles an hour in the blinking of an eye."

On Saturday, June 14th, 1947, Johnny Bliss played his first game for New South Wales against Queensland, at the Sydney Cricket Ground, before a crowd of 39,709 spectators,the home side winning by 29 points to 15, with Bliss scoring twice. As reported by (http://nla.gov.au/nla.news-article18030614) The Sydney Morning Herald of Monday 16th June 1947 "Features of New South Wales back play were the determined sprinting of right winger Johnny Bliss,................." This was the first of six games for New South Wales for which team he scored nine tries over a five year period.

The British Rugby League clubs had recognised the gift that Johnny Bliss had for the game early in his career and the following (http://nla.gov.au/nla.news-article49353895) appeared in the Brisbane Courier Mail on Saturday 15th February 1947 :-

Winger Bliss Gets Big Offer Sydney, Friday— One of the biggest offers ever made by an English club to an Australian player has been received by Rugby League winger, Johnny Bliss. The offer, from Halifax Club for a four-year contract, includes a £1000 sterling signing-on fee and £5 a week, in addition to match wages. Match wages are £7 a win, £6 a draw, and £5 a defeat. Bliss is to make a definite decision in the next few days. Halifax recently offered Bliss a contract with a signing-on fee of £950, but he rejected it. Bliss has now received three offers from English clubs. Last year, he refused to accept a contract with Huddersfield.

The Australian flyer didn't take too long to consider his response to what was certainly a superb offer at the time and just five days later on the 20th of February 1947 the Brisbane Courier Mail (http://nla.gov.au/nla.news-article49364214) covered the story with:- **Footballer Rejects English R.L. Offer** Sydney, Wednesday.— Speedy wing three-quarter, Johnny Bliss, has rejected an offer to play with an English Rugby League team. Bliss told the Manly-Warringah District Rugby League Club honorary secretary of his decision today and said he would be training with the club to-morrow night. Apparently, at that time "Blistering" Johnny was still competing in his beach sprinting and playing Rugby League as an amateur, a situation which was explained by the same newspaper a month later on the 20th of March (http://nla.gov.au/nla.news-article49341401):- **Bliss Will Turn After Beach Run** - Johnny Bliss, of Sydney, fastest sprinter seen on Australian beaches for years, will have his final races at the national surf carnival in Southport at Easter. Bliss, who is also a brilliant Rugby League winger, will then turn professional in both football and running. He is considering a lucrative offer to play league in England next season and will also compete as a professional foot runner. Without a peer in beach racing, Bliss' giant strides over the sand have captured the imagination of thousands of surf carnival spectators. He will race in the beach sprint and relay at the carnival in Southport. Bliss has signed with the new Manly-Warringah Club, in the Sydney league competition this year...........

The great speedster may have considered offers to play overseas but he never made the trip, much to the disappointment of spectators in England who would, no doubt, have seen him as a massive drawing card wherever he played.

His pace never in doubt, in August 1947 Johnny Bliss' sprinting ability was reported in The Sydney Morning Herald (http://nla.gov.au/nla.news-article27895088) on Monday 11th :- BLISS WINS SPRINT - State winger Johnny Bliss easily won a 110yds race for Rugby League players at Brookvale Oval yesterday. The race was staged by the Manly Junior League. In football togs and carrying a football, Bliss beat J. Walsh (Manly) by two yards, with J. Hickey (Western Suburbs) third, in 11.3s.Note the football togs (including boots) and carrying a football! The ball was certainly not a piece of equipment that could be carried in one hand. Neither are we talking synthetic running tracks. So, arguably we are talking here of a performance which immediately translates to 10.27 seconds for 100 yards on grass in rather heavy football boots and using one arm only! Contrast his performance with those at the Sydney Olympic Park Centre on 15th September 2010, some 60 plus years

later, when the NRL fast men took part in a 100 metres event with Usain Bolt as an onlooker, starting blocks, synthetic track surface, all in athletics gear including spikes, all able to use both arms – no football being carried. The event was won in 11.1 seconds by Wallaby Lachie Turner with fellow union player John Grant runner up at 11.15 seconds. The first NRL player was in third place – Jarryd Hayne who clocked 11.2 seconds ; Josh Morris, Ben Barba, Nathan Gardner, Matt Lewis and Greg Inglis all followed in 11.44, 11.45, 11.77, 11.99, and 12.48 seconds respectively. In football gear, carrying the ball, on grass, no starting blocks, "Blistering" Johnny Bliss ran the equivalent of an 11.23 seconds 100 metres. Enough said!

Back On The Beach,almost 18 months later, Bliss won a 100 yards handicap race in which he was giving starts of up to 14 yards and within weeks of that contest he found himself the subject of an investigation which was covered by The Sydney Morning Herald of Wednesday 2nd March 1949 (http://nla.gov.au/nla.news-article18105508), as follows:- **Surf Body Inquires Over Bliss** - Rugby League three quarter Johnny Bliss has been called on to certify he is not a professional footballer. He has been asked by the Surf Life-Saving Association for a statutory declaration that he has not received money for playing football. The association has also asked three Rugby League clubs to certify if any money was directly or indirectly paid to Bliss. The clubs are Manly-Warringah (of which Bliss is at present a member) and his former clubs, North Sydney and Balmain. The association claims it is taking the action to safeguard the interests of members of the Amateur Athletic Association, who compete in beach sprints.

Amateurs are not allowed to compete, knowingly, against professionals. The inquiry will determine whether Bliss can compete in the beach sprint and beach relay at the Australian championships at Bondi on Saturday week. A statutory declaration to the S.L.S.A. from a member of Queenscliff and Bronte Clubs alleged that Bliss had received money for competing in a foot-race at Brookvale Oval.

Bliss has lodged a counter statutory declaration denying this.....................

Via (http://nla.gov.au/nla.news-article18110099) just over a month later, on 6th April 1949, the same newspaper reported :- **Amateur Status Confirmed** - A special committee of the Surf Life Saving Association has confirmed the amateur status of Manly-Warringah Rugby League winger, Johnny Bliss. The committee reported to a meeting of the SLSA, last night that no evidence could be found of Bliss having received money for playing football. A copy of the committee's report will be sent to the Amateur Athletic Association.

(**Author's Note**: *I found myself subjected to a similar set of problems, just over ten years later, when I made the mistake of signing amateur forms for a professional rugby league club.*)

His reputation continually building on Saturday 16th September 1950 Johnny Bliss was crowned as the game's top sprinter when he won the 100 Yards Sprint Championship by an amazing 11 yards clear of the opposition. It is also recorded that in the early 1950s

Bliss officially clocked 11.1 seconds for the 110 yards distance, wearing full football gear and carrying the ball ; this was backed up by an even more meritorious performance of 9.9 seconds for 100 yards under the same conditions – fantastically fast!

Take away the ankle protective but restrictive boots and the ball, introduce running spikes, starting blocks and an acceptable running track, even cinder, and what would this man have been capable of is anyone's guess. Mine is that he would have certainly been Olympic standard as a sprinter.

At his peak Johnny was said to be the fastest white man in the World. If we take 1948-1952 as the period when he would have been at his best, the foregoing statement is worthy of examination :- Generally, at the top level of the sport of athletics within the period considered, 9.5 seconds for 100 yards was being run on a fairly regular basis with a couple at 9.4 and a World record at 9.3 seconds by the USA's Mel Patton. For 100 metres the scene was generally 10.3 seconds with the World record at 10.2 seconds held jointly by Jesse Owens, Harold Davis, Norwood (Barney) Ewell all USA ; Lloyd La Beach of Panama, George Lewis of Trinidad & Tobago and Emmanuel McDonald Bailey of Great Britain. The 1950 Empire Games (Commonwealth) held in Auckland, New Zealand, had three Australians filling first, second and 4th places in the 100 yards final, namely John Treloar (9.7), William De Gruchy(9.8) and Alastair Gordon(9.9) seconds.

From my knowledge of other rugby players times in full football gear on grass and, in certain cases, carrying the ball, I know I am safe is stating those times clocked by Bliss were worth around half a second faster on even a grass track in spikes etc., for I do know the actual times clocked in genuine track races by such athletes at athletics meetings. Apart from his Rugby League sprinting contests,where his talent had become glaringly obvious, and from which it was suggested to him that he might like to try pure track sprinting and aim for a 1948 Olympic selection for his Country, Johnny never pursued that course of action. It had been said by Australian Amateur Athletic Association officials that he had the potential to easily break "evens" without any further training. He could become an Australian track star. **My own previously stated opinion is that Johnny Bliss would have undoubtedly been Olympic standard.**

"Blistering" Johnny Bliss, just some of whose host of talents I have mentioned, eventually worked for the Fabergé and Christian Dior companies in the areas of toiletries and perfume. He conveyed the reflection that, like many Rugby League players of his era, he would happily do it all again and for nothing.

Johnny was only 52 years old when he passed away and taking all of the above into account, may well have been every bit as good as that statement – fastest white man in the World.

BOLTON Dave: (1937 - 2021)

This superb athlete played for:-

Wigan – 300 games 127 tries
Balmain Tigers – 78 games 5 tries
Blackpool Borough – 5 games.
Lancashire – 2 games.
Great Britain - 23 games 9 tries.

A member of two Ashes – winning squads, Wigan's and Great Britain's automatic choice for the stand-off half berth in the late 1950s and early 1960s, Dave Bolton could adequately be described as mercurial. He could break defences of any opposition in the twinkling of an eye, Dave would vanish into thin air. If he took the

(Photo Supplied By Dave in 1996)

ball, as on some occasions he was forced to, at a standing position, it mattered little, for this true flying stand-off had already anticipated what the defence was up to and he would be off the mark like an Olympic sprinter, often never to be stopped or even touched on his run to the line. **Dave Bolton, in my opinion, ranks as possibly the fastest ever in his position and imagine the opposition's problems when he linked up with Alexander The Great (Murphy) at Test level.** Dave was a winner of championships both in England and Australia, the latter whilst playing for Balmain Tigers in the Grand Final against St. George in 1969.

Dave Bolton was inducted into the Balmain Tigers' Hall of Fame in 2005 and in 2008 was awarded the Clive Churchill Medal for his performance in that win over St. George in the 1969 Grand Final.

BOSTON William John: (1934 -)

The National Library of Australia's assistance in obtaining the image of Billy Boston is gratefully acknowledged.

[Reference-: Daily Telegraph (Sydney NSW) 1931-1954.

19 May 1954 -League Record Tipped

Trove(nla.gov.au)/https://trove.nla.gov.au/newspaper/article/248839194?searchTerm=billy%20boston]

At age 17 Billy Boston scored 17 points out of 32 in the Boys Clubs International Wales versus England. During that period of his career, he represented Welsh Schoolboys XV and Welsh Youth XV plus Neath RFC and did captain the Boys Clubs XV. **For many the arguments and discussions about who was the greatest ever wing three-quarter to play either code of Rugby have only one answer and there the discussion ends - Bouncing Bi!ly B.** Many clubs were seeking Boston's signature when, as a teenager, the Cardiff born winger was running in tries for The Royal Corp of Signals team during his National Service. In one Army season he scored 126 tries! That's right, it's not a misprint - 126

Billy Boston training at Sydney Cricket Ground Tuesday 18 May 1954

tries! It is reported that Wigan had actually signed the Welsh Wonder in March 1953 but had kept the signing under wraps until they unleashed his athleticism in an "A" team game against Barrow in 1954, when 8,000 spectators turned up to watch his debut at Central Park. He spent the next 15 years at Wigan, scored a club record 478 tries in 488 appearances. He finished his career at Blackpool Borough before retiring in 1970. He also represented Great Britain in the team that won the 1960 Rugby League World Cup. With only half a dozen first team games under his belt he was chosen for the 1954 tour to Australia and New Zealand. A tremendous crowd puller, he did not disappoint the selectors who had put their faith in such a young athlete, and he returned a tour try - scoring record of 36 tries. Billy played 31 times for Great Britain and twice for Other Nationalities. **With well over 500 tries in his career, he is one of an elite few. A fearsome crash tackler at around the 15 stone (95 kg) mark eventually and close to 6 feet, he possessed lightning acceleration, great pace, and the agility of a ballet dancer and, in my mind, was the greatest signing The Riversiders (Wigan Warriors)**

have ever made. An athlete who, like few others, brought the crowd, home or away, to its feet every time he was in possession of the ball. He had one facet that could arguably put him above any winger ever to play the greatest game and that was his ability to more than fill other positions in the team. Wigan even once considered putting him in the pack!

As I've said, Boston possessed great acceleration and pace, but my abiding memories of this great winger are from games against Barrow when, on one occasion he took the ball some 70-80 yards out and scored in the corner, leaving a trail of, if memory serves me correctly, seven bodies lying along the touchline. This scoring feat was actually recorded by a photo in the local paper. On another occasion he was faced by Barrow winger, 6 ft. 3 inches tall and 15 st. 9 lbs. (99kg) of muscle, "Tosh" Roper whom he ran over, as it were, to score. On the way back from scoring, he patted "Tosh" on the head and helped him up from the pitch where he was lying, perhaps in disbelief of what had just occurred. I believe that Billy Boston from Tiger Bay would be in most people's top three wingmen of all time.

A statue of Billy Boston with Clive Sullivan and Gus Risman was unveiled in 2023 at Landsea Square in the Cardiff Bay area of Cardiff; at Wigan in Believe Square there is a statue of Boston on his own; at Wembley Stadium one with four other legends of the game – Eric Ashton, Martin Offiah, Alex Murphy and Gus Risman. **Undoubtedly one of sport's greatest ever players in any code, he scored a total of 571 tries in his career in 564 appearances, making him the second highest try scorer in rugby league history. He is an original inductee of the British Rugby League Hall of Fame, Welsh Sports Hall of Fame, and Wigan Warriors Hall of Fame, and was appointed Member of the Order of the British Empire (MBE) in the 1996 Birthday Honours lists for services to the community.**

BROGDEN Stan: (1910 – 1981)
"Broggy"– Lightning Acceleration

This 10stone 10lbs (68 kg.) and 5ft 8inches (1.73m.) tall flying machine was one of the most talked about players ever to appear in the Australian press when he toured Australia with a Great Britain teams in 1932 and 1936. **He was a constant thorn in the side of all opposing defences, who found his lightning acceleration, devastating pace, and ability to evade tackles very difficult to handle.** "Broggy" had 15 caps for England 4 tries and 16 for Great Britain, 3 tries. He registered 155 tries in his club rugby career.

Here was a truly legendary player, equally at home as a winger, centre or stand-off, who played for Leeds, Bradford Northern, Huddersfield, Salford, Hull, Rochdale Hornets and St Helens.

Saints Heritage Society reported that

[Photo from Daily Standard (Brisbane, Qld.), Wednesday 3 June 1936.]

"This classy Centre played whilst on loan from the Hull club. His abilities shone through as he scored four tries in four games in September and October 1944. This haul included a hat trick in the match against Oldham............... One of the quirks of the war years was the potential availability of star players for other clubs as a result of their postings in the military. Saints were delighted to secure the services of one of the greatest English players of the inter-war years when Stan Brogden made himself available. A lightening three-quarter, who would very often take part in professional sprinting competitions............. Beginning his career with Bradford Northern, he was signed by Huddersfield for a one thousand pound fee in 1929, where he made 156 appearances, scoring 90 tries. In 1934 Leeds paid a world record fee of £1,200 to secure his services. He later joined Hull and had further spells at Rochdale Hornets, Bradford Northern and Salford. He won every honour at club level and was a seasoned international, being selected for two Australian tours in 1932 and 1936. What a pity that he never played for the Saints. A true rugby league legend!"

After both the 1932 and 1936 Test Series in Australia (in 1936 incidentally Brogden was in his prime aged 26) followers of the game "down under" said that "Broggy" was, without doubt, the fastest Englishman they had ever seen on their grounds.

I well remember my father relating to me about the exceptional pace that Brogden possessed and that he was a Powderhall Sprinter, who was always handicapped out of a chance of winning the famous event. I have heard several accounts about times he was capable of over 100 yards but never one that would enable me to establish other than that he was so fast he had never been given a mark at Powderhall that would have enabled him to figure in the final. **A contact of mine from some 25 years ago, who actually saw his first Rugby League match in 1931, said that in all of his 65 years watching the game up to that time, without a doubt, Stan Brogden was the fastest of them all. Great tourist wings Alf Ellaby and Alan Edwards were both reported by my contact as saying that when Brogden broke through a defence, unless you were right with him, you may as well not bother because he would leave everyone for dead. From a standing start he was tremendously fast.** Eyewitness accounts of Brogden's speed, certainly in the 1930s, portray a superb athlete with absolutely electrifying pace which would split any defence, or "system" purporting to stop him, into ragged confusion and on many occasions did just that.

Regarding his Powderhall history consider the following information on the classic professional sprint in the days when he was reputed to be at his best: The contest was a 130 yards handicap and between 1929 to 1940 inclusive it was won by athletes running off various marks from "scratch" to 19 yards. Glasgow's "Clyde Built" Willie McFarlane, who beat the handicapper twice, ran his second win off "scratch", in 1934, running virtually 3½ yards inside "evens" when he clocked 12.66 seconds, the equivalent of 9.74 for 100 yards.

From 1929 to 1933 inclusive the race was won in times 12.0/12.56/12.44/12.88 and 12.13 seconds from marks of 14/8½/9/8½ and 7 yards respectively and for anyone to even dead heat with the winners of the event, from "scratch", in those years he would have had to produce sprinting of the equivalent 100 yards times of 9.23/9.66/9.57/9.91 and 9.33 seconds respectively. From 1935 to 1940 a similar situation obtained, with a "scratch" man, who may have had visions of winning, needing to produce sprinting of the order that equated to 100 yards times of between 9.52 seconds and 9.66 seconds just to dead heat; the exception being 1937 when a 10.05 seconds for 100 yards ability would have seen a "scratch" man able to have dead heated for first place. In amateur championship sprinting during that same period 9.4 seconds for 100 yards was the World record, only a few athletes had bettered 9.5 seconds ; the Commonwealth (Empire Games) 100 yards was being taken in 9.9/10.0 and 9.7 seconds. So, when you consider the above, it is

little wonder that someone of Stan Brogden's undoubted ability was said to have been always handicapped out of a chance of winning ; he would have had to produce considerably faster than the better than "even time" he was reputed to have run ; in fact in some of those Powderhall finals he would have had to generate World record pace to have stood a chance at a mark anywhere near "scratch" and in Edinburgh at New Year! There weren't many about who could produce that kind of pace Worldwide, never mind in the UK ; it's likely that most sprinters in that period running off near back marks never had a chance. **Perhaps this was truly the case with Stan Brogden. In my opinion, one thing is certain – the marks that Brogden, according to anecdotal evidence, received at Powderhall, eliminated any chance he had and a similar situation at The Stawell Gift in Australia would likewise have seen him go out in the heats.**

*[**The Gift** - In Australia professional foot-racing is said to have begun in the gold-mining days. The miners raced against each other, often in a one-to-one match-race situation on a handicap basis for the gift of a gold nugget offered by the local publican or mine owner.*

It was at this time that the main sprint race came to be run over the Sheffield distance of 130 yards, regarded as a true test for professional sprinters. This sprint distance originated from the Sheffield Handicap event in Yorkshire over 130 yards in which the winner was presented with a purse of gold. The metric equivalent of 120 metres has been used in gift races since the mid-seventies.

*The 'Mecca' of professional foot-running in Australia is **The Stawell Gift Carnival** which has been held during Easter for over one hundred years. Along with Scotland's **Powderhall Sprint**, it is recognised as one of the two most important and oldest professional sprint handicaps in the history of athletics professional or amateur.*

***Many rugby league players**, international athletes, footballers have participated in the event which attracts thousands of visitors.*

The Stawell Gift has a long history dating back to 1878 and remains the most important event in Stawell's sporting calendar.

The event is held over the Easter holidays at Central Park in Stawell, Victoria.

The Gift is the 120 Metres Handicap Race run on natural turf unlike international games such as the Olympics. The final is held on Easter Monday.

Aside from a place in Australian sporting history, the winner takes home a A$40,000 winner's cheque.]

Broncos- A Flying Duo
"Pearl" (Steve Renouf) (1970 -)
"The Dell" (Wendell Sailor) (1974 -)

Queenslanders who played for Australia's stand out club Brisbane Broncos at the same time.

[Illustrations by the late Brian Miller]

Steve "Pearl" RENOUF, originating from Murgon Juniors and Wondai, this Brisbane Bronco was considered by many to be Australia's premier missile in the '90s. A native Australian Aborigine of close to 6ft (1.83m.) in height and weighing in at little short of 14 stones (89kg.), Renouf was the most marked man in their game between 1989 – 1999 because once launched he was not caught.

He was well respected Worldwide. **His greatest weapon was his extraordinary acceleration, backed up with the kind of pace that saw him credited with a 10.7 seconds 100 metres.**

142 tries in 183 appearances for The Broncos plus 43 tries in 59 games for Wigan and 16 touchdowns in representative games – 11 of which were in 11 games for Australia displayed his talents.

Wendell "The Dell" SAILOR,with an uncanny resemblance in his style of play to the legendary Great Britain winger Billy Boston, powerful to the extreme, elusive with undoubted pace, this 6ft 3inch (1.92 m.) and 16 stones 10 lbs. (106 kg.) athlete had a 10.9 seconds clocking for 100 metres and plied his trade between 1992 and 2001. For The Broncos and then St. George Illawarra "The Dell" registered 127 tries, 110 of which total were for The Broncos in 189 games. Representing Queensland, The Indigenous All-Stars and Australia he produced a total of 24 tries. Twenty one of these tries were for Australia at the rate of 1 per game. The 1994 Kangaroo tour of Britain was Sailor's first taste of the game at such an elevated level and he came as the youngest member of the tour party. Powerful to the extreme and elusive with undoubted pace coupled with true defensive ability, (he was formerly a full back), prior to selection for the Tour party he had only managed a regular place in the Broncos first grade squad midway through the 1994 season and hadn't played State of Origin football. In 1998 he played Rugby Union for Leeds Tykes and scoring 15 tries in 13 games.

"The Dell" did appear for Leeds Rhinos also, in trial games, and Wigan also showed considerable interest, but he decided to stay with Brisbane Broncos.

BURGESS Bill: (1939 -)
"He Could Catch Pigeons"

The finest natural athlete I have ever seen, I actually went to school with Bill and competed with and against him over many years at school, for club and at Northern Championship levels in sprints and relays. **I have no hesitation in stating that had he concentrated on athletics as a career, he would definitely have sprinted for Great Britain.** As it was, Bill's father was a great League forward who had captained England and toured Australia, so it was no surprise that he chose Rugby as his sport. Burgess signed for Barrow in the early 60s from Union, where he had represented Furness RUFC and Fylde RUFC as well as Lancashire County and began a career in League that culminated in him being transferred to Salford. **During this time he was assessed as the Best Winger in The World by no lesser authorities than David Watkins and Alan Hardisty.** In his days at Barrow, it is arguable that the club had the fastest pair of wingers ever to play for a rugby league club at the same time, for on the other wing to Bill was Powderhall exponent Mike Murray. Defensively, Burgess was no one's fool. Many opponents will have felt the strength of his tackling. On attack, Burgess scored tries which, in my opinion, no other winger I have ever seen would have scored. The reason for this was his ability to beat man after man on a touchline run of say only 20 yards with no room to manoeuvre, but his electrifying acceleration and amazing ability to alter his pace just at the right moment would see him run a straight line and leave several defenders grasping thin air. **Long distance tries were no problem for this flier for given half a yard he was uncatchable.** To illustrate the difference between a sprinter playing rugby and a rugby player who can sprint, I remember Burgess chasing and catching Alf Meakin who played for Leeds and Blackpool, over approximately 75 yards on Craven Park. Meakin was an Olympic Sprint Relay athlete and had a time of 9.4 sec for 100 yards to his credit. **Winner of many sprint races both over 100 yards and 220 yards, Bill's best performance on the track in my opinion was in 1957 on a grass track that had endured heavy rain all day when he was victorious by almost 6 yards over some very good sprinters in a time of 10 seconds dead. Such was the surprise at the result in the bad conditions, yet it emerged he was actually timed at**

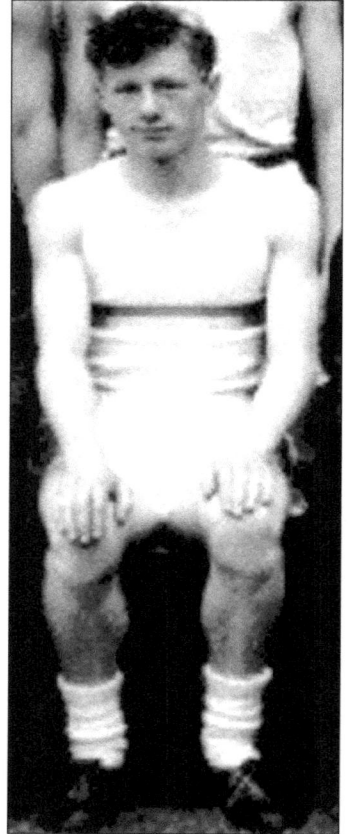

9.9 seconds. (The timekeepers rounded up the time to the 10 seconds.) The track was remeasured, and it was found to be about three quarters of a yard over distance!

Bill scored 179 tries in 222 games for Barrow, his hometown club ; eventually played at International level on many occasions starting with Barrow, with which club he gained most honours, then further honours with Salford. Bill played 14 times for Great Britain, scoring 8 tries and 3 times for England scoring 3 tries. He also represented Lancashire County at Rugby League. His three England R.L. caps were awarded for games against France and Wales and his 14 caps for Great Britain R.L. were against France, Australia, and New Zealand. On the 1966 tour of Australia and New Zealand he played in 5 test matches and scored 3 tries.

I would have loved to have witnessed Bill in the major professional sprint classics - had he been a participant. I have already stated that had he concentrated on his sprinting, at the expense of playing rugby of both codes, he would have run for Great Britain. Of that I have no doubt whatsoever. In our hometown of Barrow-in-Furness, Lancashire (as it was then), England, during the 1950s there was a profusion of good sprinters and amongst them was a standout duo. Bill was one of the pair and future Powderhall winner and British Champion Mike Murray was the other. In 1956 at Plymouth, Bill finished second in the prestigious English Schools Track & Field Championships, over 220 yards, to the sprinting phenomenon of the time, John Young, about a year and a half his senior and who that year took out the Amateur Athletic Association Junior Men 100 and 220 yards titles plus the Senior Men 100 Yards title. Young went on to play for England and the British Lions at Rugby Union on the wing.

Looking back now at 1957 when Bill was credited, (almost a quarter of a century later), with a 9.9 seconds clocking for 100¾ yards on a treacherous grass track it becomes obvious that his effort was more likely to have been worth 9.8 or even 9.7 – and in such bad conditions. Take it from me, this athlete was running in mud! Had he contested the Powderhall New Year Handicap in 1957 he would have taken part in a historical event ; it was the last time the race was run over 130 yards and British Champion Walter Spence (Albert Grant) of Blyth was taking part in his fifth Powderhall final. The accolades associated with the win that year went to another Blyth, Northumberland, sprinter J. Ball, who incidentally, had been prepared by Spence (Grant). Into a strong headwind, Ball clocked 12.45 seconds from the 7 yards mark. To have put Bill Burgess in that final would have seen an experienced sprinter of an outstanding reputation, well known in the North of England and thus over the Border in Scotland not, in my opinion, receive any favours from the handicapper and be expected to run off somewhere around the 4 yards mark at best. He had no problems with endurance so 130 yards would have been right up his street. Certainly, capable of 3 yards "inside", to have matched Ball he would have had to produce a run 1½ yards "inside" from a handicap of 4 yards. Such an effort, I am convinced, he was eminently capable of generating.

Yes - Bill Burgess could catch pigeons!

CARLTON Frank: (1936 - 2009)

"Carlo" In the 1956 R.L. Challenge Cup Semi-final against Barrow.
[By kind permission of Alex Service - Saints Heritage Society www.saints.org.uk/]

Frank Carlton was also known by the nickname of "Carlo". He was born in Blackbrook, St Helens, Lancashire. He was fortunate enough to tour twice, in 1958 and 1962 as a member of an Ashes winning party on both occasions, winning caps – one for England against France in 1956 and two for Great Britain against New Zealand in 1958 and 1962. Frank was a sprinter for Sutton Harriers and on Everton F.C. books before signing for St Helens RLFC in 1953. **Credited with circa 0.5 yard inside "even time" over 100 yards, "Carlo" indeed had a reputation as a track sprinter.** He was already a seasoned Saints wingman when selected for his first tour. Frank was a dangerous and extremely fast attacking force with a muscular, if slim, physique and from signing until 1960 Frank scored 129 tries in 156 appearances. **Arguably Carlton scored the most important try that a Saints team ever registered when, in 1956, he scored at Wembley, from half-way to seal the club's first ever success in the Challenge Cup competition with their victory over Halifax.** In the 1954/55 season. Frank registered two hat-tricks against

Rochdale Hornets and was Saints top try scorer with 33 tries. The following season saw him register a career best of 40 tries with three hat-tricks against Barrow, Liverpool City and Swinton plus an outstanding 4 try total against Bradford Northern in the Challenge Cup. This hat-trick merchant was at it again in 1956/57 season against Blackpool Borough and Rochdale Hornets plus another 4 try exhibition against Huddersfield. In 1957/58 Hat-tricks were again down to the name of Frank Carlton against Oldham and Warrington.

Frank finished as Saints leading try scorer on three occasions. This consistency enabled him to be selected for the 1958 Touring Squad to Australia where he made the Test team on one occasion. Furthermore, Frank won two Lancashire and one England cap in his time with the Saints. He also played against the Australian touring side on November 24th. 1956 when the Saints inflicted a record defeat on the tourists by 44 points to 2.

A serious leg injury almost put paid to his career. In fact, with Saints, it appeared he had been written off, but in came Wigan and signed the flier. **He then showed renewed enthusiasm and confidence to repay the faith placed in him, scoring 95 tries in 123 games between 1960 and 1965, for Wigan and being selected for the 1962 touring party.**

Frank Carlton is an inductee in Saints Hall of Fame with, in Alex Murphy's opinion, the accolade that this fine athlete was the best locally born winger he had seen.

CASTLE Frank: (1924 – 1999)
"High Powered and Streamlined"

Frank Castle – "High Powered and Streamlined" :

Not quite as fast as "Mallard" – the Doncaster, England built World speed record holder for steam locomotives, but he may just as well have been considering the number of long distance tries he scored against class opposition that simply couldn't handle his electrifying pace. The great Australian, Clive Churchill would, I believe, have borne testimony to that statement.

This exceptionally fast athlete was born in the late spring of 1924 in the Midland Counties of England. As a young man in National Service, he played a lot of rugby in the Middle East and, after his demobilisation, he eventually found himself playing for the **Coventry Rugby Union Club** which was the top team in the Rugby Football Union and for Warwickshire County from where he had trials for England.(Castle had even filled the stand-off / fly half berth for Coventry before taking the professional ticket.) **John Butler, the Club Historian at Coventry**

Typical shot of the fastest of them all - Frank Castle.

He translated track pace on to the rugby field better than any other player I have seen in over three quarters of a century supporting Rugby League.

Rugby Football Club, recalled his Father taking him for the first time to see Coventry play "circa 1947/48" with Castle in the side for which he *"played for a relatively short time after the war as a wing three-quarter of some pace".* **It was a period when, as John says** *"Frank caused a bit of a stir, although in modern times that would not be so.............The stir he caused was by turning professional & moving to Barrow Rugby League. Without TV etc. little was heard of him subsequently when of course in those days turning pro was considered not the done thing with players not being allowed to return to their old club & surroundings."*

Apart from anything else, his obvious pace was going to attract the attention of Rugby League clubs and he played a trial for Leigh RLFC in 1948. Barrow Rugby League Football Club, a northern outpost of the game, also approached the flyer and he

succumbed to the club's offer, signing on the dotted line in September 1949 for a reported £1000, the equivalent in today's spending terms of circa £42,000. Just a few days after turning professional Frank Castle made his debut in Rugby League against the mighty Bradford Northern Club and this raw, ex - Union player, in early October at Barrow's Craven Park, registered his first League touchdown from the halfway line, demonstrating awe inspiring pace which had the crowd eagerly anticipating what just might be to come in the future from this truly special athlete that their club had signed. In a Barrow team that had many internationals at the time, Frank flourished and scored many fantastic tries that relied on his special pace and defence - deceiving in and out swerve.

*In their book **"Keeping The Dream Alive"**, Messrs Huitson, Nutter and Andrews (2008) expressed the following poignant lines which describes this athlete perfectly:-*

"In the so called 'Golden Age' of Rugby League in the late 1940s and 1950s, when crowds were at an all-time high, the wingmen of the day came in three very specific categories. They were very fast, exceptionally fast or Frank Castle!"

In his one club career in League, which lasted the better part of eleven years, this exceptionally exciting winger scored 281 tries for Barrow RLFC during an epoch when the game was graced by some of the greatest and fastest wingmen ever to play either code of the sport. In fact, there were centres and scrum halves in those days that would have given anyone playing today more than a run for their money. Two of the numerous great tries, reliant on his fantastic speed off the mark and ground eating acceleration, that he registered for Barrow that stand out in my memory occurred against Salford and Leeds when, on both occasions, he came inside around about his own 25 yards line to take a pass from the great stand-off Willie Horne and scorch through the defenders and under the posts without a single hand being laid on him ; in the case of the score against Leeds he even received applause from some of the Leeds players. A third stand out effort was his 101 yards score against the almighty Wigan —with Barrow grimly defending the Duke Street end of their Craven Park ground and a decision made to start an attack from that precarious position by flinging the ball out wide to where that massive and great centre Dennis Goodwin on receipt quickly handed it on to Frank Castle who received the pass one yard behind the Barrow line. Castle set off and at a stunning pace had beaten the Wigan cover inside 25 yards and was in free space as he sped past the players' entrance. *[In those days there was plenty of cover defence in the game of Rugby League to beat, not like today with usually a single line defence which once penetrated by someone with real pace spells TRY.]*

The Barrow flying machine headed infield and made a bee-line for the waiting Wigan full back and at about the half way line he showed him the ball, as he often cheekily did to defenders, then swerved outside and away to the posts.

A genuine length of the field try and again not a hand laid upon him – his pace had seen to that - enough said!

[At the time, Barrow RLFC had two great wing three-quarters, the other being "Gentleman "Jim Lewthwaite. They were every bit as good as their legend! Of contrasting styles, both Frank and Jim were devastating exponents of wing play. Also, that fantastic exponent of pace, swerve and side step, of the 1940s and 1950s, Brian Bevan was season by season prominent and whenever Warrington played at Craven Park, caused the pre-match anxious query from many – "Is Bevan playing …?" so dangerous was the table topping flying Aussie try machine. Yet during Bevan's first eleven seasons in the UK (1946-47 – 1956-57) the only English players to top 50 tries in a season were Frank Castle (1951-52) with 52 touchdowns, one more than Bevan, and then in 1956-57 Jim Lewthwaite crossed for 51 tries.

In the whole of Bevan's career, no Englishman bettered those individual performances of the Barrow wingers. With "Prince of Centres" Phil Jackson and the mighty Dennis Goodwin, both internationals, playing inside Lewthwaite and Castle respectively and being fed by the unmatchable Willie Horne and his international scrum half Ted Toohey, the three-quarter line was undoubtedly one of the best ever to play for any club Worldwide.]

Frank played at Wembley three times in Challenge Cup Finals, winning once; in representative football he played for England against France, Other Nationalities and Wales with a 5 tries total ; he also played for Great Britain against France in international matches and represented a victorious Great Britain in all three Tests of the Ashes series against Australia in 1952 scoring, in the First Test at Leeds, one of the greatest international tries I have ever seen that could arguably be said to be the score that started the rot as far as Clive Churchill's otherwise super Kangaroo team was concerned, causing into the bargain the great Australian full back to virtually tackle the corner flag whilst Frank produced a, rare for him, side step and raced over the line. Frank registered two more tries in the Second Test at Swinton. He also scored six tries in the first five games including the First Test for the 1954 British Lions in Australia but received a serious leg injury that certainly finished his tour and almost put paid to his career. *Incidentally "Castle Seen As Star Of R.L. Tour" was the headline in the N.S.W. Newcastle Sun on Friday 12ᵗʰ March 1954 where the great Australian winger Brian Bevan said that Frank Castle, of Barrow, would develop into the drawcard with the English Rugby League team in Australia. Bevan said, "Castle's speed on the left wing will make him the flyer of the party."*

Frank told me that the Barrow Club could never tell him how many tries he scored although we both knew it was around the 300 mark ; with the helpful information provided by Messrs Huitson, Nutter and Andrews in their work **"Keeping The Dream Alive"** and from other sources I reckon a minimum of 295. **In all my decades watching** this great game of Rugby League, a senior sprints coach for 52 years, over 20 as an active sprinter, I have never seen a faster man on a rugby field, in full gear, carrying the ball, than Frank Castle. Why do I make such a statement ? Simply because here was an athlete who had a reputation for pace that was able to actually demonstrate this great asset on the field of play during a long career against some of the fastest men ever to play the game. As you read on, I ask you to consider the scene today and I'm sure you'll agree that there is not the same standard of pace amongst the modern wingmen except for the odd one or two. So, who were some of these speed merchants that Frank Castle came up against ?

"Peter 'Sammy' Henderson"- Huddersfield Rugby League Club's flying All Black, 5th in the final of the 1950 British Empire Games 100 yards and a Bronze medallist in the Sprint Relay and credited with a best time over 100 yards of 9.7 seconds was part of a formidable duo in a glorious Fartown back division. The barnstorming Lionel Cooper was on the other wing!

On Saturday, February 28th 1953, the second round of the Challenge Cup, at Huddersfield's Fartown ground saw the home team take on Barrow RLFC in a game which the latter were defeated, but at the same time, a game which underlined the pace of Castle when he scored from 45 yards out and with Henderson as level as one could wish, he ran away and left the Kiwi further and further behind with each ground - eating stride to the point where Henderson actually gave up the ghost and eased off.

In his prime, Australia's Team Of The Century (1908-2008) wingman, Kenneth John Irvine, who was hailed as "The Fastest White Man In The World" including both amateur and professional sprinters, was actually even better than that and was indeed "The Fastest Man In The World". The nineteen year old flyer came to the UK with the touring 1959 Australian Kangaroos, already having a reputation for tremendous pace, which status was more than verified by Brian Bevan who complimented Irvine on his running after he had scored an 80 yards try against the Australian wonder winger who had played for over a decade at Warrington. In scoring two tries in the game in which Barrow beat the tourists 12 - 9, Frank showed the Aussie speedster a clean pair of heels. For one of the scores, Irvine gave up the chase and he had started virtually level with the Barrow Express. Consider also that I am also talking about a 16 year difference in age between the two players, Castle being 35 at the time. **All things considered, I would have to say that my money would have been on Castle, at the time, to rank amongst the very fastest men in the World in any sport, for his age.** These were just two occasions of many that I could mention. Frank Castle was not the best wingman I have seen but he was certainly the most exciting.

[Other considerations regarding all of the players of that era were, the heavier boots (although Frank Castle's were specially made and light in weight - I had a pair), also the restrictive shoulder pads and, many would argue convincingly, most of all the playing surfaces with which they had to contend.]

Ken Jones was a champion sprinter – representing Great Britain, a Silver medallist in the 1948 Olympics 4 x 100 Metres Relay and at the 1954 European Championships in the same event ; Bronze medallist in the 220 yards at the 1954 Commonwealth Games. He played for Wales RU for ten years beginning in 1947.

[Incidentally in that Olympic relay squad one of his colleagues was Jack Gregory the man that Frank told me had kept him out of the 1948 Games.]

The great centre three-quarter Lewis Jones once said of Castle when comparing his speed with that of Ken Jones, whom he had partnered in Welsh R.U. teams, that with Jones you could give him a pass and then run alongside in support waiting for a possible return inside. However, with Castle that just wasn't on as no sooner had you given him the ball than he was under the posts. Another Rugby League great, Willie Horne who, let's face it, had seen an abundance of talent and pace in his illustrious career, also said that Castle was the fastest player he had ever seen.

I only saw Frank Castle caught on the field of play, twice, - the occasions were, once by the excellent Ralph McCarten and once by "The Borroloola Flash" Wally McArthur and, don't forget, Castle had the ball under one arm!

[Note that when I use the word "caught" I mean chased down by a player actually running in the same direction, not cut off by a player running across field which, of course can happen to any pace merchant no matter how fast he is.]

Just consider a few of the great flyers that Frank Castle played against- Stan McCormick; Brian Bevan; Tom Van Vollenhoven; Peter Henderson; Wally McArthur; Ralph McCarten; Frank Carlton; Ken Irvine, etc., all of them with recorded factual reputations as top class sprinters.

Not a big man at around 5ft.9ins.(1.75m) and 12 stones (76kg), he had tremendously powerful thighs and calf muscles which obviously were of a great help in providing that lightning speed off the mark. **I had more than one talk with Frank about his pace and found out that, apart from being in line for a place in the British Sprint Relay Squad for the 1948 Olympics, he was very proud of an achievement that, even today, would be considered outstanding when he clocked "evens" no less than 4 times in one afternoon - once each in heat, semi and final of the 100 yards and he was also clocked in his relay leg.** Frank had a best time of 9.8 seconds for the 100 yards. When related to the facts that between 1946 and 1953 Emmanuel McDonald Bailey took out no less than seven Amateur Athletic Association Championship Titles at 100 yards, with an average winning time of 9.73 seconds, and the remaining title in 1948 was taken by John Treloar of Australia in 9.8 seconds, the reader gets a strong indication of the undoubted class of Frank Castle on the running track. This is where I believe he had the advantage over his contemporaries in League, he translated that pace onto the field of play, in football gear and carrying the ball, better than anyone I have ever seen. One thing that is absolutely certain is that any winger currently playing at a professional club would be hard pushed to get within yards of Frank Castle at his astonishing best.

High Powered and Streamlined he may have been, *but Frank told me that he didn't enter the Powderhall or other professional sprints because he felt his chances of a decent handicap mark were nil. He was probably correct in that assumption.*

Nonetheless, in the self-appointed role as a Discretionary Handicapper, I am going to consider how he may have fared in the 1948 Powderhall New Year Sprint and the Stawell (pronounced Stall) Easter Gift in Australia of the same year. Walter Spence (Albert Grant) of Blyth, Northumberland had taken the spoils in the 1947 Powderhall and was a competitor again in 1948, albeit having been penalized back to the 2 yards mark from the 5½ yards he had the previous year. This handicap did not prevent the lightly built 24 year old Blyth man reaching the final for the second of five occasions on which he would achieve that feat. In that 1948 major professional sprinting event in the UK, he had to contend with the opposition from, ex Guardsman in the British Army and a contrast in physique to Spence, J.S. Wilson of Musselburgh, East Lothian, Scotland, running from the 9½ yards mark, A. Mitchell of Kelty, Fife, Scotland, off 7½ yards and, from south of the Scottish Border, S. Georges of Mickley, Northumberland, England, off 5 yards. The punters fancied the chances of the 1947 champion as he started at odds of 5 to 4 with Georges at 7 to 4, Wilson at 7 to 2 and Mitchell rank outsider at 25 to 1.

The Mickley sprinter S. Georges was value for his second favourite ranking as he finished in 2nd place, but Wilson and Spence exchanged places with the former, who had also competed at Powderhall before but without success, claiming the victory by inches from Georges, with Spence finishing a further foot behind in 3rd place. The winner clocked 13⅜ seconds, a time which probably reflected the conditions. The Midlands Express – Frank Castle, yet to sign for Barrow Rugby League Club and still an amateur, a possible Olympic selection for the "Austerity Games" of 1948, would have provided substantial interest at such a carnival of professional sprinting as Powderhall. How could he have matched up to those finalists that year ?

Well, I've already stated that here was the fastest man I've ever seen on a rugby field, (in full football gear, carrying the ball), in 77 years.

I only twice saw him caught by two individuals who, in anybody's book, would be termed International Class if not indeed World Class at the time and many were the occasions when this fine athlete showed a clean pair of heels to others of the aforementioned, recognised standards of International and World sprinting.

Now in this 1948 Powderhall final we have a sprinter who would also be claimed as World Class and he was also the reigning champion – Walter Spence (Albert Grant). He was capable of times over 100 yards, echoed from his times at other distances on grass and cinder tracks in various competitions, of certainly circa 9.6 seconds. Frank Castle, a potential Olympian, would not have been recognised as a "novice" where he would have been handicapped in my opinion anywhere in the region of the 7 to 7½ yards mark, but based purely on times relative to the two sprinters of 9.6 (Spence) and 9.8 (Castle) seconds respectively, I estimate that the man from the Midlands was capable of matching the Northumberland Express from a mark of 4½ yards i.e., receiving two yards from Spence. Allow that mark to advance just a half yard to 5 yards and I would reckon that Frank Castle would have taken Spence and also Wilson in that final.

To register "evens" four times in the same afternoon proved that Frank Castle would have had little trouble in dealing with heats and semi-finals of any sprinting event. Would he have survived at Stawell in 1948? Given a decent mark I'm sure he would have. The question is what would such a mark have been? There was a great deal of successful sprinting experience amongst those competing and though, like at Powderhall, he could not be treated as a "novice", I see no reason why discretion would not see him allocated a mark of 5 yards from which I am convinced he would have matched Tom Brudenall of Ballarat running off 8 yards, even though giving him a 3 yards advantage, and from 5 yards which would have been back mark in the final, Frank Castle could certainly have taken The Stawell Gift in 1948.

The most exciting wingman I have ever seen passed away in August 1999.

CLEARY Michael: (1940 -)
A triple Australian International
Rugby Union, Rugby League and Athletics

This Wallaby Wing commenced his Test career with the National team against Fiji in 1961 and played a total of six Tests before signing for South Sydney Rabbitohs Rugby League outfit, presumably receiving no money, in order to maintain amateur status so he could compete in the 1962 Commonwealth Games at Perth, Australia.

[By the way, a move which would not have worked in his favour in Great Britain as it would strictly have broken the Laws of The Amateur Athletic Association. I am surprised it was not so in Australia.] My own personal experience would verify this.

Mike had been an outstanding schoolboy sprinter who would represent his country and, in those Commonwealth Games, he was awarded **the Bronze Medal** in the 100 yards final some 48 hours after the actual race. This was in consequence of the track referee asking to review the photo finish of a keenly contested final. Cleary clocked 9.78 seconds in that race against a 1.8 metres per second wind. He had clocked 9.4 in winning his heat with a 3.4 metres per second following wind. **The New South Wales flyer had at least two more claims to fame as a top class sprinter - via his photo finish victory, on a wet grass track, over the great Ken Irvine, with 10,000 fans looking on at Sydney's Wentworth Park Greyhound Complex in 1964, at the same time picking up a £1000 purse and clocking 9.7 seconds for the 100 yards and with his 1966 130 Yards Australian Professional Sprint Championship win.**

His rugby league career was marked by his reputation for being both elusive and fast and he toured Great Britain in 1963. At this time, along with Reg Gasnier, he featured in a televised race against none other than Eddie Waring, revered Rugby League commentator. Eddie was driving his car! My research indicates that Cleary in Rugby League (having already represented his country in Rugby Union), had a scoring record of:- 5 tries in 8 appearances in Test matches between 1962-65; 28 tries in 22 appearances for Sydney and New South Wales between 1962-69; 88 tries in 125 appearances for South Sydney Rabbitohs and Eastern Suburbs between 1962-71.

Mike eventually entered politics, becoming Minister of Sport in New South Wales and In 1992 was awarded "Officer Of The Order Of Australia" in the Queen's Birthday Honours list recognising his distinguished service to the New South Wales Parliament. For his achievements as a Kangaroo, he was awarded the "Australian Sports Medal" to commemorate his contribution in making Australia a country of sporting excellence.

[There have been many "Fastest Man In Rugby League" events over several decades, the results of some of them a little bit suspect because of the lack of entry of some of the big names in the sport. This scarcity of talent in entries, when it came to proof of how fast any individual with a big reputation was, certainly occurred in England – they chose not to enter. This was probably because they wished to maintain that big reputation, often overstated. I have seen a report that highlighted Aussie Dave Irvine in such an event, which he won, then was criticised as not being the fastest because Michael Cleary and Ken Irvine were not competing. Had they been in the event there's still no guarantee that either of them would have come out victorious. Dave Irvine was noted as having certainly caught Mike Cleary from behind on the rugby field anyway. There is no doubt of the outstanding ability of this New South Wales athlete.]

How would Michael Cleary have fared at Stawell and Powderhall ?

Cleary was a schoolboy sprint champion who developed into an International.
A regular in Gift events after he turned professional, Cleary was amongst other Rugby League speedsters that could not win the popular Canberra Gift. Ken Irvine who Mike Cleary conquered at Sydney's Wentworth Park Greyhound Complex in 1964 was another. A reminder of that famous Greyhound Complex victory came in 2007 when the inaugural running of the Mike Cleary 100 Yards Sprint with prize money of AU$5000 was staged at the same venue. Cleary was of course the 1966 Australian Professional Sprint Champion. How then would he have fared at The Stawell Easter Gift? Well, in 1962 The Gift over 130 yards was taken by L.N. Beachley of Rosanna, Victoria, off 8¼ yards in 12.1 seconds. Cleary was already of national prominence as an amateur. Would Mike Cleary have been given anything other than the "scratch" mark to run from? I doubt it. Could he have produced an effort better than 7 yards "inside even time" which is what would have been required to win? Again – I think not. Even off a very favourable 3 yards he would have still had to go better than 5 yards "inside". In 1966 "The Accountant From Wodonga" – the celebrated Bill Howard - took out the AU$1700 and Gold Medal for his win from 8¾ yards in 11.9 seconds. Even from 4 yards Mike would have had to improve on 7 yards "inside". Doubtful in my opinion.
What would have been the likely scenario for the New South Wales flyer had he been a competitor in the Powderhall New Year Handicap in 1962 and 1966?

In 1962, for the third of five consecutive years, the event was held at Newtongrange and over 120 yards. The period had been one of the coldest on record with temperatures recorded at Edinburgh around minus 13 degrees Centigrade and remaining sub-zero so I doubt if Mike Cleary would have found such conditions anywhere near inviting. However the final saw the great Scot, Ricky Dunbar giving half a yard to Charlie Harrison of Bedlington, a town just north of Newcastle Upon Tyne in Northumberland, with the former off 6½ yards and the latter, who would win the prize, off 7 yards. Harrison clocked an 8th ranking time, amongst those who won the event whilst it was contested at 120 yards, when he registered 11.58 seconds. So Harrison held off Dunbar, who would take out the event in 1963, and the Bedlington athlete's performance was worth 2½ yards outside "even time", which I would suggest would be attributable to climatical conditions. With Dunbar unable to take Harrison, would Cleary have had any better fortune? Considering the circumstances likely to have prevailed on the Australian International and that he may well have been fortunate enough to have received a mark around the same as Dunbar, I think he might have been capable of springing a surprise. In 1965 the event had returned to Powderhall and the following year, still over 120 yards, at which distance he would register a time only bettered by Dunbar himself at Powderhall over New Year Handicap finals, Barrow Rugby League winger Mike Murray was victorious in 11.42 seconds off 4½ yards. Dunbar in 1963 also off 4½ yards had run just 0.03 of a second superior to Murray. So where would Mike Cleary have figured in such an event?

Very low temperatures and a somewhat frozen track are the conditions he would have had to contend with but by now we are talking about a Commonwealth Bronze Medallist who was also now an experienced professional, very likely coming into the form that would see him become Australian Professional Sprint Champion that very year. Given any kind of decent mark, up to off level with Murray, the spectators may have seen one very exciting race.

Michael Arthur Cleary truly was a class athlete.

DALLAS Brett: (1974 -)
King Of The Wing

Brett entered the international and State of Origin scene in 1995.

This Queensland born flyer played for Canterbury Bulldogs, North Sydney Bears, Wigan RLFC, Queensland and Australia and at 13½ stones (86 kg.) and 5ft 9ins (1.75 m.) had devastating pace.

Between 1992 and 2006 he played for three clubs - Canterbury Bulldogs, North Sydney and Wigan. Representative honours came his way via Queensland, ten times when he registered 4 tries and Australia on six occasions with a net of nine tries in the Green and Gold.

Stories of players' speed are often misleading and sometimes baffling, even absolute nonsense and it suits the player and his club to leave it that way. Benefits arise from such illusion - increased gates for example, to see this or that flying machine. **I can assure the reader that this Australian was a true flyer and I have no doubt that Wigan fans would back me on that statement.**

The JJB Stadium at Wigan, the home of Wigan Rugby League Club and Wigan Athletic FC, (now the DW Stadium) was the scene of one example I would put forward as testament to the pace of Brett Dallas, whose ability in that regard I commented on in 1996 long before he ever donned a Wigan jersey. On Google Earth the playing area appears to be accurately measured so as to be accepted as 100 metres between try lines ; some in the game are not, although they purport to be. Brett Dallas appeared for Wigan in the right wing berth against Bradford on 1st September 2001. Wigan won the game 16 points to 10 and Dallas scored a sensational try after a chase down of a kick by one of his team colleagues. The game was played in good conditions and in that run Brett Dallas, timed by me over a "flying start" 40 metres, clocked 4.35 seconds without the ball. This run shows that the Australian was sprinting on grass and in full football gear at slightly better than "even time" pace, i.e. to be exact at 10.875 for 100 metres.

A second illustration I would submit as to the sprinting ability of Dallas took place at The Stobart Stadium, Widnes in Merseyside on 18th April 2004 when he faced Warrington in a Challenge Cup Semi-Final. Again, the playing area appeared to be accurately measured so as to be accepted as 100 metres between try lines. In scoring his 68th try for the Wigan Club he ran almost the length of the field but I have used the part of that effort that was straightest, i.e. after he had beaten most of the opposition tacklers. The game was played in good conditions and clocking Brett over a "flying start" 40 metres and a "flying start" 60 metres, carrying the ball, I came up with times of 4.45

seconds and 6.6 seconds, which pace converts to 11.125 and 11 seconds dead for 100 metres, in full gear and carrying the ball.

The Wigan Club was obviously conscious of the pace of Brett Dallas and others in the squad, so much so that it was reported, at the end of 2004, that they were going to make use of ex Olympic sprinter Dennis Mitchell's coaching on a training trip to the USA.

Having no official time for this Australian King Of The Wing, although I have seen both 10.9 and 10.8 seconds down to his name for 100 metres, I would suggest that when compared with other rugby sprinters/athletes, whose official performances I do know, and using the two examples I refer to above, I would reckon that on a track he would have been well inside "evens"!

In 1993 Brett did actually win a 75 metres sprint and the title of Fastest Man In League, (Australia), conquering into the bargain the favourite Lee Oudenryn, (who had a 1992 win over Martin Offiah before a Parammatta v Great Britain game), and pocketed in the region of AU$4,000. The race was run as part of the proceedings at The Botany Bay Gift Gala.

As mentioned previously, I have clocked Brett Dallas over "flying start" 40 metres and 60 metres on the rugby field in match conditions, both with and without the ball. I have seen in over 75 years many sprinters, rugby players of both codes, of all standards.

I offer my considered opinion that Brett Dallas had what it took to be in the top drawer, with possibly a 9.8 /10.7 for yards/metres.

DAVIES Jonathan: (1962-)
"Jiffy"

Why is Jiffy actually called Jiffy?

www.walesonline.co.uk/sport/rugby/rugby-news/jiffy-called-jiffy-every-famous-12091048 with an article by Delme Parfitt and Anthony Woolford explained-

"We've got to the bottom of one of the great rugby mysteries.
Ever wondered why Jonathan Davies is called Jiffy? Well, the real reason is going to surprise you, we can guarantee.
You hear many theories advanced by those who claim to be in the know.
We've had: "It's because he had lightning pace...he'd be gone in a jiffy!"
We've had: "It's because he's a huge fan of the American peanut butter Jif, spreads it on his toast every morning by all accounts."
In fact, we've heard all manner of weird and wonderful explanations.
But the truth is far simpler than you would ever imagine.
When Davies joined Neath in the early 1980s someone in the dressing room began to call him Jiffy, for no apparent reason.
There had actually been another player at The Gnoll for years who had been christened with the same name but he had left.
For reasons unknown the Jiffy tag stuck to Davies like a limpet. It's never gone away and it never will. Perhaps he should explore a trademark."

The Welsh rugby genius at 5 ft 9 in (1.75 m) and 12 st. 4 lb (78 kg) throughout the 1980s and 1990s in Rugby Union for Neath, Llanelli, Cardiff and Wales, scored 74 tries. Between 1985 and 1997 he won 37 caps in the Union game. In 1988 Wales won the Triple Crown in which success he took part.

Turning to Rugby League, lured by Jim Mills and Dougie Laughton he signed for Widnes for £230,000 (purchasing power today of circa £740,000). He scored 135 tries representing Widnes, Canterbury Bulldogs, Warrington, North Queensland Cowboys, Wales and Great Britain from various positions in the back line – full back, wing, centre and stand-off.

He played for The Chemics (Widnes) as a centre in their 1989 World Club Challenge victory against the visiting Canberra Raiders. Selected to play for Great Britain during the 1989–1992 Rugby League World Cup tournament he went on to play his part in the

Widnes 24–18 victory over Salford in the 1990 Lancashire Cup and their 24–0 victory over Leeds in the 1991–92 Regal Trophy Final.

Moving on to Warrington in the 1993–94 season he won RFL's Man of Steel Award. Then he played the 1991 NSWRL season for the Canterbury-Bankstown Bulldogs and in his 14 games registered 7 tries.

On his second visit to Australia in 1995 playing for North Queensland Cowboys he is well remembered for his length of the field try against Newcastle Knights.

1995 saw him return to Union with Cardiff and on a guest appearance on A Question of Sport he was asked what the biggest change was in his return to the Union game. Davies replied: *"It's the first time I've been cold for seven years. I was never cold playing rugby league".*

There were many associated with Rugby League who, at first, thought that the Welsh International fly half was not big enough for League or likely to be tough enough. Suffice to say that Widnes had the good sense and foresight to sign him and since that time, even though he was transferred to Warrington, he proved to be arguably the most valuable buy ever to come out of the Valleys, with the possible exceptions of Lewis Jones and Billy Boston.

For the purpose of this work, I consider Jiffy as a centre three-quarter.

As far as pace is concerned, perhaps the best example I can give is that of the Davies match winning try at Wembley in the First Test of the 1994 series between Great Britain and Australia. He showed that day that there would be very few recognised speed merchants in the history of the game who could catch him, as he out-paced Australian fullback Brett Mullins who was himself very fast indeed. Jiffy was named Man of The Match.

Davies was somewhat of an enigma, as far as I am concerned, regarding his apparent physical attributes for sprinting, appearing to be short in the body but with a stride length that would be more suited to an athlete six inches taller. He used his legs to the best advantage with a high knee lift and extremely good driving action, both natural facets of his running which many pure track athletes strived for and never achieved. **Yes, it would be a very confident man that would bet against Jonathan Davies in a race of centres of any era.**

Jiffy became an MBE in the 1995 New Year Honours list for services to Rugby League Football. Then in the 2015 Birthday Honours list, he was promoted to OBE for his work in voluntary and charitable services to People with Cancer, in recognition of his work as President of Cardiff's Velindre Cancer Centre.

Jiffy a Class Act

DRUMMOND Des: (1958 – 2022)
Jamaican Superstar

Des Drummond was born in Jamaica in 1958. Predominantly a Leigh and Warrington player in England, The 12 stones (76 kg.) 5 ft7ins. (1.70 m.) Drummond did play a short time in Australia in the mid-1980s. **In Lancashire in particular and in the English Rugby League scene in general Des Drummond was an idol who was not only incredibly fast but also just as tough as he was speedy.** Between 1980 and 1988 he claimed 24 caps for Great Britain, including being a 1984 tourist to Australia. In a notable 21 year career which began at Leigh RLFC in 1976 he went on to play for Warrington RLFC and his other English clubs – Bramley, Workington Town, Chorley, Hunslet, Prescot Panthers and Barrow – being almost 40 years old when he signed for the latter. Drummond registered 141 tries for Leigh in 280 games and for Warrington 69 tries in 182 games. For Workington Town he touched down on 32 occasions in 71 games. **Overall in that 21 year club career Des was scoring virtually a try in every two games he played. He scored "tries of the season" on several occasions for Leigh and Warrington.** Representing Lancashire in 4 matches Des scored 3 tries; England in 5 games, 1 try; Great Britain in tests and tour matches 17 tries in 34 appearances.

Anyone who saw Des Drummond in full flight would recall just how exhilarating his pace was and testimony to that was how this extraordinary athlete took Rugby League to the forefront of national television coverage when, in the 1983 B.B.C. Superstars competition he provided the nation with a record breaking performance in the 100metres clocking 10.85 seconds. **The time was comparable with full-time track and field athletes who would compete in the following year's Olympic Games.**

This international pocket battleship would vie for the title of the most dangerous, pound for pound winger, in the game's history. Lightning fast off the mark. and with an elusive style coupled with strength that found many confident defences wanting, he was a great crowd pleaser throughout his long career. Des Drummond ran "inside evens" over 100 yards and, in my opinion, could "fly" over virtually any terrain be it muddy rugby fields or synthetic tracks. Like many others from previous eras, Des Drummond would be a match in pace for anyone playing Rugby League today.

EDWARDS Alan: (1916 - 1987)

It is recounted that when Alan Edwards joined Salford from Aberavon R.U. club in 1935, his new team mates felt that he wouldn't last very long in the League code. Apparently his physique appeared to leave something to be desired. However, as proved to be the case a decade later with another unlikely physique, that of Brian Bevan, the Welshman became a great success in the game. With a fantastic fervour for rugby, Edwards was lightning fast from the mark and on taking a pass would be at top speed in no time at all. His sidestep from the left foot is legendary and he achieved this with absolutely no loss of pace.

A slim speed merchant to say the least, he was selected by Wales within two months of turning pro and scored in the Welsh win over France. Talking about speed on the field of play and carrying the ball Alan was and still is revered as one of the fastest ever to play Rugby League.

Don't forget we are considering a young man at the age of just 19 when this was taking place and only months after signing he was on tour with the victorious 1936 Great Britain squad in Australia and New Zealand and finished up as leading try scorer with 21 tries. Over 300 tries scored in a career saw him also guest for Dewsbury and signed by Bradford Northern from Salford; he formed a duo with Barney Hudson at Salford which made them one of the most feared pair of wingmen in the game's history.

Alan won 18 caps for Wales in 1935 –1948 while at Salford and Bradford Northern and won caps for Great Britain while at Salford in 1936 against Australia (3), and New Zealand (2); then in 1937 against Australia (2). He was the youngest member of the 1936 tour party.

The Salford side was becoming increasingly stronger and with rain falling on a heavy ground when the Aussies made a visit on tour in the U.K. Salford defeated the Australians 11- 8 at The Willows, Saturday October 30th, 1937, with Alan registering an important touchdown. On 7th May in 1938 at Wembley Alan was a member of the victorious Salford team that beat Barrow 7 - 4 in the last minute of the Challenge Cup Final before 51,243 spectators. This was an outstanding victory since Barrow had recently hammered Salford 31 – 0!

[My Father often related stories of this Salford team and I was lucky enough to meet Barney Hudson and Gus Risman when I played a trial for Salford in1957.]

Edwards, Osbaldestin, Hudson, Gear, Risman, Watkins, Feetham are familiar names even now.

In the Championship Final at Maine Road against Castleford on May 13th, 1939, Alan scored the winning try in an 8 – 6 victory before 69,504 spectators. That season saw him score hat-tricks against Barrow, Oldham and Batley in a 33 total for the season. In the 1948 Challenge Cup Final at Wembley when Wigan proved triumphant over Bradford Northen by 8 points to 3 before a World Record crowd of 91,465 spectators Alan scored the Bradford Northern try.

Alan Edwards remains one of a celebrated few Welshmen that scored over 1,000 points in Rugby League.

ELLABY Alf: 1902 - 1993

In March 1926, this tall, Prescot born, elegant ex-soccer player made his debut for St Helens and started a career which, even today, sees him hailed as the finest wingman to play the game between the two great World Wars.

Alf Ellaby's career totals in try scoring are, to say the least, impressive for any era and for his period with St Helens I have seen various sources quoting differing totals, therefore I will quote the information provided by Alex Service Saints historian.

"Ellaby flew in for 278 touchdowns in 290 appearances for the Saints, figures exceeded only by Tom van Vollenhoven and Les Jones. Dubbed The Hat-trick King, he notched three tries on 31 occasions for the Saints and was the first player to score a half-century of tries in a season at Knowsley Road, with 55 in 40 matches in 1926/27. Alf toured Australia with both the 1928 and 1932 Great Britain squads and made 13 Test appearances overall. Capped by Lancashire on 19 occasions, he touched down 17 times for the Red Rose County. Ellaby scored after just 30 seconds in the First Test against Australia at the Sydney Cricket Ground in 1932 and he captained his country in the first-ever international against France in Paris in 1934."

[His 55 total tries for Saints in the season 1926/27 stood as a club record until the advent of the Springbok, Tom Van Vollenhoven, who exceeded that total in 1958/59.]

Representing Lancashire, England, Other Nationalities (against Wales), Tour Matches plus in Tests and other representative games Alf scored 76 tries then with Wigan a further 90 tries. He was the first Saints player to register 6 tries in a game, when he played against Barrow in 1932. Born in St Helens, Ellaby was a wing flier who totalled just shy of 450 tries in a career that saw him transferred to Wigan and back to Saints where he finished off his time on the field of play. His position as all-time top try scorer in the game's history held until Brian Bevan, in 1954, superceded Alf's total. A cartoon in Saints Archives depicts Ellaby as **"The man who could give a start to the Royal Scot "** (an extremely fast express train).

A great favourite, even in Australia, (**"The Tin Hare"** as they dubbed him), where he toured twice. Alf Ellaby could and did put thousands on the gates at grounds wherever he played.

As Alex Service reports:- *"Skill and guile was always the best way, as he showed in the international between England and Wales at Wigan in 1928, when he did the unthinkable and scored a hat-trick against the great Jim Sullivan! His performance that day showed what a truly great performer he was, using change of pace to great effect and the ability to stop dead in his tracks to totally bamboozle the most famous full-back in the world!"*

With a reputation of being able to take a wide pass, a high pass or pick up of the ground at top speed Alf Ellaby, a member of Saints Past Players Hall of Fame, was certainly a unique athlete.

FIELDING Keith: (1949 -)
A 'Superstar'

Keith, born in Birmingham became a Loughborough College Physical Education student. During that period he joined Moseley Rugby Union Club where his abilities were obviously nurtured to the point where he became a County player and in the 1968-69 season gained his England cap against Ireland. Against France and Scotland that season and in the following season he gained further selection facing Ireland and France again plus South Africa. In the first fixture with France, Keith scored a try. He was soon to join Salford Rugby League Club but in the lead up to that momentous point in his career the flying machine became England R.U. top try score with a 39 total and represented his country on a further four occasions. Keith had also represented The Barbarians and seemingly had a particular competence with Rugby Sevens; in the much acclaimed Middlesex Sevens in 1970 he scorched in for a magnificent 11 tries.

Another eye-catching illustration by the late Brian Miller.

Signed by Salford in May 1973, in his first season this truly flying wingman, who no less a figure than David Watkins recognised as the fastest he had ever seen, set up a Salford season total for tries of 46, which still stands. (He actually registered 49 tries including international games). Defences didn't give Fielding much room intentionally, but he really didn't need more than the odd half yard to outpace any defence in the land as his Salford career total of 253 tries displays.

Fielding won caps for England:- in 1975 against France; in the 1975 Rugby League World Cup against France, Wales, New Zealand, Australia, Wales and France; in 1975 against Papua New Guinea. In October 1975, Keith equalled the England record for most tries by an individual in an international match when he scored four against France in Bordeaux. Representing Great Britain

he won two caps in 1974 against France; then against France and Australia in the 1977 Rugby League World Cup.

Reputed to have run the equivalent of 9.6 seconds for 100 yards, his instant acceleration and overall pace was displayed to great effect on many occasions against solid defences and also during his appearances in the **B.B.C. Superstars** series in 1977.(In the Superstars competition Fielding clocked 10.9 seconds for 100 metres.) Keith has been reported as stating that he would have beaten Martin Offiah for speed, a declaration with which I would most certainly agree.

The Canberra Times on Wednesday 6 March 1974 reporting on the upcoming tour of The Antipodes by Great Britain highlighted that **" Fielding, who played 10 times for England rugby union, is considered weak on defence, but has**

electrifying pace and is considered the fastest man in England."

The same newspaper on Monday 18 Jul 1977, when Great Britain had overwhelmed NSW Southern Division by 54-6 the previous day, recorded that

Keith, who had finished with four tries in the game, also **won the 110 metres Central Coast footballers sprint before the game.**

It is certainly arguable that, in his era, Keith Fielding was the fastest wingman in the World.

FORD Phil: (1961 -)
As Elusive As Any Rugby League Back In History

Phil Ford played Rugby Union in his native Wales for Rumney RFC and Cardiff RFC. His career took him into League onto the books of Warrington (1981) where he played 112 games and scored 57 tries, Wigan (1985) 15 games and 16 tries, Bradford Northern (1985) 107 games and 59 tries, Leeds(1988) 96 games and 50 tries, Salford (1992) 93 games and 55 tries, Wales, 8 games plus 4 tries and Great Britain 21 games 16 tries. His career was a testimony to this Welsh flier's worth. Phil also played for a Rugby League X111 and scored a try. To many, a wing enigma, (although he could also play centre and fullback) in that he could do something out of this world one minute and then spoil his performance the next minute, **Phil had his fans and his critics but of one thing there is no doubt - he could run very fast indeed. One try he scored against the Aussies will go down in history as one of the best they ever conceded and, if memory serves me right, he hadn't a hand laid on him in an amazing, but typical Ford run, from the full back position, across and through the World Champions' defence.** The former R.U. man, never famed for his defensive qualities, was not short of guts and was perhaps most effective defensively when giving chase.

There were few, if any, that could outpace him. Phil was a tourist with the 1988 Great Britain squad in Australia. In the team that beat Australia in the third Ashes Test and was "honoured" by the hosts who nicknamed him "The Rubber Man" so elusive was he.

He was in the Welsh squad for the 1995 Rugby League World Cup.

FREEMAN Johnny: (1934-2017)
A Son of Tiger Bay

In December 1954 Halifax signed Welsh R.U. Cardiff born wingman Johnny Freeman from Cardiff International Athletic Club, for £1050 (£31,000 in purchasing power today). This son of Tiger Bay, cousin of British Empire Heavyweight Boxing Champ Joe Erskine, in those days was playing alongside Billy Boston. It is reported that Halifax originally signed Johnny as a centre, the position he had held in Rugby Union. Though I have no information on any track running this classy winger had performed, he was fast and elusive and scored many tries at Thrum Hall and on other grounds. **So effective was he as a scoring machine that he set the Halifax club record for career tries from 395 appearances providing a total of 290 which still stands today, as does his tries in a season total of 48. He was leading try scorer at Halifax for no less than 7 consecutive seasons. Not many wingers could even think of scoring a hat-trick against Billy Boston but Johnny Freeman did just that and at Central Park Wigan!**

In the book *"The Glory of Their Times: Crossing the Colour Line in Rugby League"*, Robert Gate the game's greatest historian's description of Johnny Freeman was…

"It appeared that every time Freeman got the ball he scored or at least threatened to score. Certainly the crowds began to expect miracles when he was in possession. Here was a man who could go the length of the field, who could break tackles when apparently held, who could find that extra gear, when already seemingly flat out, who could go past defenders on the inside or the outside, who would be first to any kick forward and who could pluck interception tries out of nothing. He had star quality, good looks and an effortless movement which was captivating."

No better or more appropriate testament to the great Welsh athlete's abilities could be more vital.

When one thinks of players who have approached the Rugby League record for tries in a season, held by Albert Rosenfeld of Huddersfield, with 80 touchdowns in 1913/14, one is apt to bring to mind Brian Bevan, Lionel Cooper and Tom Van Vollenhoven perhaps, but not Johnny Freeman.

Now, in 1957/58 season the Halifax flier scored no less than 38 tries in the first 20 matches and knowledgeable supporters of the game reckon he would definitely have threatened Rosenfeld's total but for a knee injury which caused him also to miss out on virtual certain selection for the 1958 British Lions tour to Australasia. That knee injury in December 1957 cut short his international ambitions and put him out of the game for a year.

Johnny did represent Wales in 1963 against France at Stade des Minimes, Toulouse on Sunday 17 February. Against New Zealand in 1955 Johnny scored a 50 yards try which helped Halifax conquer the tourists. He also appeared for a classy Halifax in Championship, Challenge Cup and County Cup Finals between 1955 and 1965.

The Tiger Bay boy's career spanned no less than 13 years at Thrum Hall and he is a Halifax Hall of Fame member.

GASNIER Reg "Gaz": (1939- 2014)

Australian Centre Three-quarter Legend – Reg "Gaz" Gasnier's Statue in tribute to his ability at Sydney Football Stadium

At 5ft 11ins (1.80m) and 12st. 10lbs. (81kg.) this exceptional athlete was ideally built for his position in the period which saw him dominate the game, certainly in the Antipodes and to a great extent worldwide.

In 269 first class games Gasnier scored 231 tries:- For St George Dragons 161 games 139 tries from 1959 to 1967; For Sydney City and Country Firsts 8 games 7 tries; For New South Wales 22 Games 20 tries; For Australia in Tests, World Cup and Tour games 78 played 65 tries.

He represented Australia in 36 Tests and three World Cup games. He was the captain of the Australian side on eight occasions between 1962 and 1967. Gasnier captained and coached the 1967 Kangaroos on their tour of Great Britain.

"Gaz "had all of the attributes required – including great acceleration and pace. **Dave Bolton remarked** *"He was a great player. Along with Eric Ashton the best centre I've ever seen. He was very fast and very deceptive. You never knew what he would do next. He'd be running straight and then veer left or right."*

NRL (ARL) Chairman Bill Buckley said "He was the greatest rugby league player I have ever seen. Gasnier had an amazing change of pace and great anticipation…….. He was without peer."

He finished his international career as Australia's most capped player, with a total of 39 caps (36 Test and 3 World Cup), a record that remained until Mal Meninga broke it in 1992. Gasnier scored 28 tries for Australia and captained the side on eight occasions.

Gasnier was selected as one of the original post war Australian game's **"Immortals"** in 1981 and in December 1981, he was inducted into the **Sport Australia Hall of Fame.**

In 1989 he was awarded **Life Membership of the St. George Dragons club**. Gasnier was appointed a **Member of the Order of Australia** (AM) in 1989 and awarded the **Australia Sports Medal** in 2000 plus, in 2001, the **Centenary Medal** having also been named (in 1992) by the Australian game's leading magazine "Rugby League Week" as **number 3 in a list of top 100 players**. In 2002, he was inducted into the **Australian Rugby League Hall of Fame**. 2006 and 2007saw him named in the **NRL Team of the 1960s and 1950s** respectively. In February 2008, he was selected as **one of Australia's 100 Greatest Players** by the National Rugby League and Australian Rugby League to celebrate the code's centenary year and in April that year was named by **New South Wales in their team of the century**. He was also named as one of the centres, (along with Mal Meninga) in **Australian Rugby League's 17 player Team of the Century.**

Nicknamed "Gaz", which foreshortened his name but also depicted the fact that he possessed great powers of acceleration and was able to develop them into considerable pace; he was at home on top of the ground or in the mud and scored many long distance tries where the fact that he had a winger outside him was purely incidental.

No one could ever pick a "World Team" without considering "Gaz" Gasnier.

GRUNDY Jack: (1926 – 1978)

A second row who played 374 games for Barrow and scored an amazing 112 tries which places him among the top 10 for the club.

Jack played 11 times for Lancashire and 13 times for Great Britain scoring 3 tries for the National side. His caps for Great Britain were in 1955 3 matches against New Zealand; 3 more against Australia in 1956; in 1957 against France another 3 caps; in the 1957 World Cup where he registered 1 try he was capped against France, Australia, and New Zealand. The great athlete had one more appearance also against France.

Balding, tall and of solid physique, Jack Grundy was a "Saint" before he played for Barrow where he featured in three Wembley Cup Finals, 1951 defeat by Wigan, 1955 victory against Workington Town and 1957 defeat by Leeds plus gaining County and Test honours as well as being a World Cup representative and winning the Lance Todd Trophy against Workington Town at Wembley in 1955. Barrow Hall of Fame inductee Jack also played in Barrow's 12–2 victory over Oldham in the 1954 Lancashire Cup Final at Station Road, Swinton, on Saturday 23 October 1954.

Jack Grundy must have been one of the best, if not the very best player that Saints ever let go to another club. A £1,000 transfer fee in 1950 took him to the Furness area. **One of the greatest second row forwards of all time in the game of Rugby League, the man had everything required in a class player. A gentleman of fair play, tough as teak, a text book tackler, a great rugby brain and to cap it all, tremendous pace. Grundy had a very natural style of running that made him look more like a back than a forward, quick strides with a high knee lift.** Many tries were scored by this "iron man" and on numerous occasions the opposition would be crying out for offside because Jack had found himself directly under a famous Jim Lewthwaite cross kick and would touch down under the posts. **Take it from me, it wasn't offside, it was pure pace from one of the fastest forwards ever to play the game that got him there!**

HANCOCK Michael: (1969-)

At 6ft. (1.83m.) and 14 st.11lbs. (94 kg.) this fine athlete with abundant pace was a great favourite with Brisbane Broncos, Queensland and Australia between 1988 and 2000. He then moved on to play for Salford, for which club he scored 7 tries in 37 appearances having finished at Lang Park with 274 appearances for the Broncos and touchdowns totalling 120 tries.

For the Maroons of Queensland Michael scored 6 tries in 16 games and as a Kangaroo he registered 5 tries in 13 games for his country.

In 1989, he made his debut for Queensland as the youngest footballer of either state to play in a State of Origin series and scored two tries in the 36–6 win over NSW at Lang Park. Also in that year, and still a teenager, he made his first appearance as a Test player on the tour of New Zealand. This early success saw Michael named as Brisbane Broncos 1989 "Rookie Of The Year". Also in 1989 he took the Dally M Award for Best Winger.

In the 1992 World Club Championship against Wigan at Central Park he scored twice in the Broncos 22-8 victory over the R.L. champions in which game the Broncos became the first Australian team to win the World Club

Illustration by the late Brian Miller.

Challenge in England. As he signed for Salford in his thirteenth season with the Broncos and after a Grand Final win he had played in the Brisbane Broncos' first five Grand Final victories in 1992, 1993, 1997 1998 and 2000.

Also in 2000 Michael Hancock was awarded the Australian Sports Medal for his contribution to Australia's international standing in the sport of rugby league.

As he left the Broncos he held the record for most appearances until Darren Lockyer surpassed his total in 2007. He remains second all-time top try-scorer for the club. In 2003, Michael was one of the first four former players inducted into the Broncos Hall of Fame. Four years later at the Broncos' Twenty Years anniversary he was a member of the squad named as The Best 20 Players to have represented the club. A year after that tribute he was named on the wing in the Toowoomba and South West Team of the Century.

This product of the Queensland and Australian system of turning out world class League players is one of the most powerful and elusive (when he decided that was the best way forward) wingmen I have ever seen. Possessing a fine sidestep, he was a Test player of some magnitude. A Brisbane Broncos regular for several seasons, Hancock was famous for generally always beating the first attempt to tackle him and with such an athlete this will spell danger to any defensive system. I suppose exciting and sometimes awe - inspiring are the best adjectives to describe this speedster who was clocked just inside "even time" and was an athletics champion who won the title of Toowoomba's Fastest Footballer in 1987.

HARDISTY Alan: (1941 -)
Mercurial Stand-Off

The swinging '60s were the halcyon days of a player who, amongst stand-off halves, I have always rated amongst the greats.

Alan Hardisty was a fine tactician, an able tackler and could swing a game for his Castleford side in the twinkling of an eye and often did. With Keith Hepworth he formed one of the game's most feared and respected half back partnerships.

Alan's abilities were, in my opinion at least, keyed to one aspect of his talent - his tremendous powers of acceleration from a standing start and a pick-up of pace so effective that once away it was virtually pointless for any defender to give chase and if he managed to make an interception, which he often did, then it was all over bar the shouting.

This unpredictable athlete played for Castleford, Leeds, Yorkshire and Great Britain and his career was littered with a fair sprinkling of honours. Castleford with Alan Hardisty won the **Yorkshire League** in 1964-65. He was in the triumphant teams that saw the club victorious in three consecutive **BBC2 Floodlit Trophy Finals** 1965,1966 and 1967.

In front of Wembley Stadium crowds of 97,939 and 95,255 Alan and his Castleford team mates took the Salford and Wigan teams to task in winning the **Challenge Cup Finals** of 1968-69 and 1969-1970 seasons.

Success followed Alan to Leeds which club he captained in their **Championship Final** victory of 1971-72. **Yorkshire County Cup Finals** of 1972-73 and 1973-74 both found Alan contributing to victories. Also in 1972-73 he was in the Leeds side that won the **Player's No.6 Trophy Final.**

Alan won 12 caps for **Great Britain** and scored 9 tries whilst for **Yorkshire County** he was to touchdown 3 tries whilst gaining his 5 county caps.

Alan Hardisty who scored 201 tries in 406 games for the club is a Castleford Tigers Hall of Fame inductee and in 2009 was rated as one of the best ever players to have graced the game in West Yorkshire.

Alan Hardisty a true legend of Rugby League.

HARRIS Eric: (1909 -)
"The Toowoomba Ghost"

I'll start this item on Eric Harris by quoting **"Forward" in the Leeds Sports Echo from January 1938** after seeing the Queenslander score four tries against Salford:-

"CLASS BY HIMSELF" - "Harris as a scorer of tries is in a class by himself; he is without a doubt, very near to being the best try scorer the game has ever seen."

Toowoomba, in Queensland, Australia, is on the top of the Great Dividing Range in the Darling Downs and a gateway to New South Wales. There are many ghost related tales linked to Toowoomba. Eric Harris was certainly as difficult to catch on the wing as any ghost. He played at representative level for Queensland and the British Empire, and at club level for Western Suburbs (Brisbane) and Leeds.

(Wikipedia.org/wiki/Eric Harris)

In **The Brisbane Courier Mail of Saturday 26th July 1930, journalist Harry Sunderland (1889 -1964)** who was also involved in the league game in many other roles throughout his career – Secretary of Queensland Rugby League and involved with The Kangaroos, Secretary-Manager at Wigan Rugby League Club, even an involvement in the promotion of the game in USA and commemorated by the awarding of The Harry Sunderland Trophy to the man of the match in UK Championship(Grand) Finals – wrote of Harris as *"Queensland's Loss - Eric Harris, the fastest runner playing Rugby League football at the present time and who scored the sensational try in the last minute last Saturday, to win for Queensland, will play his last match this afternoon for the Maroons. While nothing official has been given to the Queensland League, at a late hour last night it was learnt from another source that Harris has been given a signing-on fee of £500 to go to England with Jeff Moores to play for Leeds. In addition to this, he is to be given an appointment as a school teacher and will receive a playing fee of £6 per match for a win, £5 for a draw, and £4 for a losing match....................".*

In Yorkshire, with the Leeds Club, "The Toowoomba Ghost" became an all-time legend scoring an amazing 391 tries in 383 games for the club over nine seasons. He still holds that club's tries in a season record with his 63 scored in 1935-36 ; in

17 consecutive matches he totalled 36 tries a figure never bettered in the sport of Rugby League.

He was a favourite with the Leeds supporters and thrilled them with his phantom- like running and electric acceleration, hence one reason for the nickname. He would often leave tacklers grasping at thin air by using this acceleration whilst, apparently, being already flat out. He once scored 8 tries in a game against Bradford Northern. **Harris is acknowledged as one of the greatest wingmen of them all and, regarding his electric pace, had been credited with better than "even time" in Australia. The Toowoomba Ghost is remembered as amongst the best ten players ever to represent the Leeds Club.**

Further testimony to this Australian athlete's pace was again provided by **Harry Sunderland in the Brisbane Courier Mail of Monday 16th December 1935** when he said *"We had one really great sprinter-footballer, who was the greatest certainty ever "made" for a Gift at Stawell, or Shepparton, if he had not been so open as to run Tommy Miles in an exhibition race. This youth revealed his speed to such extent that the handicappers would not have given him the mark he was entitled to as a "maiden."*

That was Eric Harris, the tall young school teacher who went to Leeds and became one of the greatest scoring wingers in English football. Harris was the very rare exception of a tall lightly built youth who had speed and rare courage, also ability to take knocks. He was in football young enough to learn when to try to run for the corner, instead of short punting to beat his defence, or whether he could foil his opposition with an elusive change of pace. Harris had the pace to move at half speed with a shorter stride and then lengthen it to accelerate and fool his antagonist. It's a rare quality."

[The fact that Tommy Miles of Bundaberg, Queensland had won the Stawell Gift in 1927 and arguably put up an even better performance in 1929 when he won his heat clocking 8 yards inside "evens" off "scratch" and was considered to be the greatest sprinter since Jack Donaldson and Arthur Postle, exemplifies the standard of sprinting of which "The Toowoomba Ghost" was capable, as does the fact that the same Tommy Miles set a professional World record for 110 Yards in 1928 when he clocked 10.3 seconds. Miles also became World Professional Champion in 1928.]

To have given such as Tommy Miles any kind of opposition, be it in an "exhibition" race or not, rates Eric Harris as having tremendous pace. He had been credited with better than "evens" in Australia and did have success in competitive sprinting. In 1929 when he was circa 20 years of age and was just over a year from going to England to play for Leeds RLFC the Toowoomba Ghost was considered to be the fastest player in Australian Rugby League.

(The Stawell Gift is Australia's major sprint challenge.

The Shepparton Gift likewise was a similar event albeit in 2023 it had just been revived after a 23 year absence from Victoria's sporting calendar.)

Peter Smith in the *Yorkshire Evening Post* of 26th March 2020 reported that:- Eric made his debut for Leeds as a 21-year-old against Featherstone Rovers at Headingley on September 27, 1930, scoring twice and played his final match at home to Bramley on September 2, 1939, and scored again. Harris scored 63 tries in 1935-36, which was a club record and registered eight tries against Bradford Northern in 1931 and seven in another match against Acton and Willesden five years later. In 1935-36 he registered a total 36 tries in a British record 17 successive matches. Twice a Challenge Cup winner and try scorer on both occasions, Eric was a member of the Leeds side that claimed the Yorkshire Cup and Yorkshire Championship each on five occasions.

He became a teacher at Carnegie Physical Training College in Leeds and married a local lady. He returned to Australia at the start of World War 2.

The Toowoomba Ghost was inducted into the Leeds club's Hall of Fame in 2019. Still revered at Headingley where he averaged more than a try a game for them he is acknowledged as one of the greatest wingmen of them all.

HENDERSON Peter: (1926 – 2014)
"Sammy The Flying All Black"

Huddersfield full back, Johnny Hunter gives Peter Henderson (left) a reverse pass against Wigan in the Challenge Cup semi-final at Odsal, Bradford, 28 March 1953. Ernie Ashcroft is the Wigan player. Photo kindly supplied to me in 2012 by Dave Gronow - Huddersfield Giants Historian.

Peter "Sammy" Henderson – The Flying All Black was indeed a New Zealand R.U. All Black wingman with several Test appearances to his credit before he signed professional forms for Huddersfield. He was to form an integral part of one of the best duos of wingmen ever to arrive from the Antipodes, himself on the right wing and Aussie Lionel Cooper on the left in an exceptional Huddersfield team.

The nickname "Sammy" was apparently the idea of a team mate on an All Blacks Tour of South Africa in 1949. Peter habitually scored tries by diving at the try line and at that time the world's best springboard diver was "Sammy" Lee from U.S.A.

For those who think that some of today's backs are rather prolific, consider the spot check I carried out on the number of tries scored by the Huddersfield back division in 1952/53 with the season still 3 months to run, no less than 112 touchdowns, with Henderson having registered 31 of them. At a similar juncture in the season two years later, Henderson and Cooper had registered 85 tries between them thus proving the lasting nature of the ability of Henderson who scored over 200 tries in his career in England.

Obviously his inborn track speed was vital in such performances. Henderson was an Empire (Commonwealth) Games sprinter with a time for the 100 yards of 9.7 secs.

Born in 1926 at Gisborne in North East New Zealand, Peter Henderson's prowess as a speed merchant is even today acknowledged in The Land Of The Long White Cloud as one of the fastest All Black players in the Rugby game's history. In the late 1940s, not a big man at around 5 ft. 7 ins. tall but of stocky build at just shy of 13 stones, Peter Henderson was showing great form in the North Island's Wanganui team and was selected for the 1949 All Black Tour of South Africa where he played in all four of the Test Matches, scoring a try in one and emerged as the Tour's top try scorer with seven in his 16 game total appearances. In 1950 against The British Lions he played another three Test matches, taking his total All Black appearances to nineteen and scored a try in the last Test at Eden Park.

Peter was a British Empire Games (Commonwealth Games) sprinter and in 1950 at Auckland, New Zealand, he ran 5th in the Final of the 100 Yards behind three Australians and a Canadian. The event was taken by John Treloar (Australia), 9.7 seconds followed by William De Gruchy (Australia) and Don Pettie (Canada), both clocking 9.8, then Alastair Kinnaird Gordon (Australia) in 9.9 seconds, the same time being given to Henderson who was followed by countryman Clement Parker in 10 seconds. In the 4 x 110 Yards Relay the All Black gained a Bronze medal with his colleagues Arthur Eustace, Clement Parker and Kevin Beardsley. The squad clocked 42.6 seconds finishing behind winners Australia, 42.2 seconds and England,42.5 seconds. The fact that Henderson ran the anchor leg is testimony to his great speed. In his athletics career Peter Henderson was credited with a best time for 100 yards of 9.7 seconds.

As was the risk in playing representative Rugby of either code at the time Peter found he had lost his job whilst on the Tour of South Africa and this unfortunate consequence was a major factor in him deciding to take up the professional game of Rugby League. He signed for the Huddersfield Club in Yorkshire, England and became part of certainly one of the top five Rugby League teams I have ever seen in over 75 years supporting the game. Earning about £9 for a win was not bad money considering it would be worth over £330 today. The Huddersfield team of that period actually became known as "The League of Nations" because of the many players from overseas employed by the Club.

One of the pinnacles of his career in Rugby League was the Challenge Cup Final at Wembley Stadium in 1953 where, before a crowd of 89,588, Huddersfield beat St Helens by 15 points to 10.

For those who think that some of today's backs in both Union and League are rather prolific, the ability of Henderson saw him score over 200 tries in his career in England.

Peter also continued to play and score at International level, representing the brilliant Other Nationalities side, so named for obvious reasons.

Obviously his inborn track speed was vital in such performances.

A blight on this great athlete's career and subsequent life had been effectively placed by the Rugby authorities back in New Zealand when he turned professional. This part of Henderson's history is best seen via an article written by Chris Rattue in the New Zealand Herald of Saturday 13th May, 2006, extracts of which appear below by kind permission of Chris Rattue (2012):-

Former All Black Banned From Rugby For 38 Years:-

"......................... *There is actually nothing secretive about Peter Henderson's history. It's there in the rugby history books. But it was a double life of sorts, where sporting success was marked with a hurtful stain unfairly left by others. This sporting life was not always in such a neat street.*

He was an All Black who had done no wrong, by any normal standards, yet was ostracised by the hierarchy, or as Henderson sees it, by one influential man at the top.

"Thirty-eight-and-a-half years," says the 80-year-old Henderson, when asked for the date that he was officially re-admitted to amateur rugby, having been outcast for the sin of playing professional league.

Tellingly, the length of the draining sentence is measured down to the last half whereas the year of release is referred to without the hint of a celebratory drink.

"It started in 1950, so you work it out from there. The whole time, I held a guilty conscience, that I had done the wrong thing."...

Henderson, who was playing for Wanganui, had returned from the 1949 All Black tour of South Africa - where he played in every test - to find his job as a dental technician had gone. Touring had cost him £400 and he had lost a similar amount in wages.

Henderson switched codes after playing against the 1950 Lions, using competing interest from three English clubs to secure a deal that would score him £5500 in fees over seven years for Huddersfield. In addition, he could earn about £1500 a year in bonuses.

As an indication of this worth, Henderson and his wife Leonie were able to buy a two storey, three-bedroom house in England for just £1500.............................

On the other side of the world, in his homeland, he was classified a rugby outcast, even though no letter ever arrived from the New Zealand Rugby Union to state this or declare what he could or couldn't do.

"It seemed farcical, even at the time," says Henderson. "They were cutting their own throats. People like myself and [other 1950s league converts] Jack McLean and Tommy Lynch had something to give back to rugby but they didn't want us............................."

Henderson's black mark meant he could not coach rugby, as he wished to do at the little country club of Ngaruawahia where he farmed, or get test tickets through the Rugby Union. But it was the stigma that really hurt. His initial attempt at reinstatement involved having to organise a bizarre chain-letter of support which started with Ngaruawahia. It was sent in error by Waikato to Hawkes Bay, the venue for his last rugby match, instead of Wanganui, his last union. It missed the intended New Zealand union meeting, and his case went on the back-burner.

At times, Henderson would be persuaded by friends into official functions following internationals, but never felt at home.............................. [Officials would seemingly ignore Henderson at every opportunity]

....................The irony is that this administrative behaviour was at serious odds with the camaraderie which existed among players, opponents included, in Henderson's playing days.

Over the years, Henderson enjoyed a firm friendship with the great Welsh wing and athlete Ken Jones, via sporadic get-togethers. Jones marked Henderson in the 1950 Lions series and the final test in Auckland contained a number of famous moments involving the two.

Henderson's nickname of "Sammy" was given to him by a 1949 All Black teammate because of his penchant for diving to score tries. American Sammy Lee was a famous springboard diver at the time. Henderson produced his famous dive for a crucial try, after keeping Jones at bay, at Eden Park only to be chastised by fullback Bob Scott for not having run towards the posts.

"When you've got an Olympic sprinter on your hammer, you don't bugger about," Henderson recalled............................

It also says something of the spirit of the times that Henderson regards Jones' try in that test as his, Henderson's, greatest moment in rugby. The try, started by Lewis Jones from under his posts, and completed after a massive sidestep and 50m run by the other Jones, a 1948 Olympic Games sprint silver medallist, is a classic.

"It is my favourite rugby memory - the best try I have ever seen in my life" says Henderson...................................

[The great Welsh players Lewis Jones and Ken Jones will be referred to again in this work in relation to another great flying wing three-quarter.]

In 1989, at another post-test function, the former All Black captain and New Zealand union councillor Bob Stuart, a Henderson supporter, approached. He said: "By the way Peter, your reinstatement went through today." I looked at him and said: "Do you realise I've been waiting thirty-eight-and-a-half years for someone to say that." He just casually came out with it. Peter "Sammy" Henderson - The Flying All Black who had been banned from the game he loved for thirty eight and a half years had been officially reinstated!"

The Flying All Black Peter Henderson at his best from the sprinting point of view would have been a sight to relish at either of the big two professional classic sprints on either side of the World.

HOLLINDRAKE Terry: (1934-2015)

Over 15 years as a professional rugby league player, most of it at first team level, says something for the staying power and ability of the 16 year old schoolboy, who signed professional forms for Keighley in 1951.

Hollindrake found that he was able to cope with the pace of the established fliers of the day who, generally, played for more fashionable clubs. Easily inside 11 seconds for 100 yards, which is not Olympic pace,I know, but you just try to do it. It's still moving very quickly indeed. Hollindrake was known throughout the league as a wingman who had served his apprenticeship and was respected wherever he played. He also played centre and sometimes fullback. His efforts were rewarded on 17th December 1955 when, on the wing, he represented Great Britain against New Zealand at Headingley - Keighley's only home grown international.

His career saw Terry play for Yorkshire on 5 occasions. A career try total of 236 is testimony to his ability. Terry was also an accomplished goal kicker with circa 550 successes and a points total (tries and goals) in his first class appearances over 1000points.

This fine athlete represented Keighley (221 matches), then in 1960 transferred to Hull F.C. for £6000,(purchasing power today circa £150,000) followed by Bramley, returning to Keighley in 1969 for a further 26 games.

Terry Hollindrake had a sidestep that had to be seen. He wrong - footed many a would be tackler with this ploy. He was an exceptional fast all-round wingman in an era that had a profusion of great wingers.

Another Keighley winger was **John Rock** who also played for Bramley and of R.U. background. Rock was not a prolific try - scorer but, in the 1950s had the distinction of winning a R.L. Players Sprint Championship. He could turn on blistering pace and was the scorer of some spectacular touchdowns which were testimony to his professional sprinting activities. **Rock was said to be an "even timer".**

HORNE Willie: (1922 – 2001)
The Unmatchable Willie Horne.

Willie Horne's lightning speed off the mark has taken him into the clear in the 2nd Test against Australia in 1946.

Two trial games with Oldham then 16 years with Barrow culminating in 461 appearances, 112 tries and 739 goals.

14 games for Lancashire with 4 tries.

14 games for England – 3 tries.

8 matches for Great Britain and 2 tries.

Willie captained Barrow in three Challenge Cup Finals – one win in 1954-55 ;

A Lancashire County Cup Final win in 1954-55 ;

Lancashire, England and Great Britain and in 1952 led the team to an Ashes winning series. He toured Australia twice 1946 and 1950.

The absolute greatest stand-off half I have ever seen play either code of the game! I would rank Wally Lewis and Alan Hardisty in the same class but Willie Horne was second to none and one of the sporting world's true gentlemen. So many defence splitting breaks would see the Maestro of off halves go for five to fifteen yards and then look, apparently with some anxiety on occasions, for support from his team. **His ability to make such breaks was down to amazing speed off the mark and an unmatchable rugby brain.** Typical of this Freeman of the Borough of Barrow-in-Furness was his lightning responses to any game situation. **So, what if this inborn gift was not backed up by Olympic overall pace, Willie's movement from a standing start was so excellent that no defence could really ever master him even at the close of his long career. Many top class sprinters, of any era, would have envied the Great Britain Captain's starting ability!**

At his best Willie was recognised universally as the greatest player in the world. Ted Verrenkamp, who was president of Brisbane Easts from 1977 to 1986, was awarded life membership of the Queensland Rugby League, one of only 14 men handed the honour in 102 years and when I was in talks with him at Brisbane's Easts Club, Ted's first words were – "Do you know a man called Willie Horne?".

Willie, a member of the Barrow Club's Hall of Fame, was inducted into the Rugby League Hall of Fame in 2014

HUDDART Dick: (1936-2021)
Dick Huddart is a Rugby League legend
the use of the adjective being entirely appropriate

As a player he registered with Whitehaven,(64 games 34 tries); St Helens,(209 games 76 tries); St. George (78 games 16 tries); Cumberland,(11 games 4 tries); England and Great Britain (16 games 2 tries).

In October 1958,after completing the memorable tour to Australia, Dick signed for St Helens from Whitehaven. This was a great blow to the Cumbrians for whom the six footer was a lethal attacking weapon. After starting out his career as a junior in back positions, the pace he had as a natural talent was obviously going to stand him in good stead when he moved into the pack as a professional.

In my opinion, the fastest forward of any era, Huddart knew one way forward, the shortest distance between two points, and was renowned for splitting defences, at all levels of the game, with devastating and sustained bursts of pace. A Lance Todd Trophy winner, Dick Huddart played at Test level and toured Australasia on two occasions, finally emigrating down under and playing for St. George (the most successful club side of all time) in their 1966 Grand Final win.

(Many thanks are due to Alex Service and Saints Heritage Society who supported my research into Dick Huddart including Dick's photograph.)

Today, great forwards are in good supply, but none compare in the capability to devastate the opposition with pace and power as one Dick Huddart.

HUDSON Barney: (1906 – 1971)
A Red Devil

I never saw Barney Hudson play but I did have the good fortune to meet him at Salford in 1957,when I played a trial for the club, as he managed the "A" team for Gus Risman. I suppose he must have been in his early 50s at the time and he was a big man. It was easy for me then to visualise the stories of this fast, barnstorming wingman that my father had related to me.

Hudson was one of those loyal athletes who signed for and stayed with one club.*(Except for guesting with Dewsbury 1941 – 1943)*. From an unusual source, the North East, Hartlepool Rovers R.U. club, Barney Hudson signed for "The Red Devils" in the late 1920s and played until 1946.

(He was one of the players who successfully toured in France with Salford in 1934, during which tour the Salford team earned the name "Les Diables Rouges")

Apparently, he only knew one way to the line and that was straight forward irrespective of who or how many blocked his path and, like many other wingers of strong physique, he tended to get faster the further he went. Couple this strong fast runner to a remarkable sidestep and a very powerful hand - off, both of which Barney Hudson possessed, and you can imagine watching the forerunner to the Cooper / Boston era. Hudson registered 282 tries for Salford.

Guesting for Dewsbury between 1941 and 1943 he scored 46 tries.

Lancashire County Cup Final wins came his way against Swinton in 1931 followed by a great series of triple wins against Wigan in 1934,1935 and 1936.

Guesting,for Dewsbury in the 1942 Yorkshire County Cup Final, Barney again was a winner.

Rugby League Championship Final victories as a member of the Salford team came facing Swinton in 1933, Warrington in 1937 and Castleford in 1939.

For Dewsbury he gained another Championship Final winning medal in 1942.

In 1938 Barney was in the victorious Salford team that beat Barrow in the Challenge Cup Final at Wembley.

For Dewsbury he had one winning Challenge Cup Final medal from the game against Leeds which was played in two legs in 1943.

His international caps were gained for:-

England against Australia in 1934;

against France, and Wales in 1935;

against Wales, and France in 1936;

against Wales in 1938.

For Great Britain:-

against New Zealand in 1932;

against Australia in 1933;

against Australia in 1936;

against New Zealand in 1936;

against Australia in 1937.

In 40 appearances in the National jersey (Great Britain/England) Barney registered 39 tries.

This prolific athlete scored a career total of 367 tries although I have seen a figure of 372 quoted – circa 370 not bad in my opinion!

IRVINE Kenneth John: (1940 – 1990)
Bear & Sea Eagle - Fastest Man in the World

The great Kangaroo winger pictured in June 1962 as Great Britain play Australia in the First Rugby League Test at Sydney Cricket Ground. (GB 31 – AUS 12). Ken Irvine scored in this Test. The anxious GB players pictured are Dave Bolton, Eric Ashton and, on the ground looking up, Billy Boston.
[Photo permission to publish granted in 2012 by:
Mitchell Library, State Library of NSW. [d7_12645] is gratefully acknowledged.]

His sprinting ability is a matter of record. In March 1963 Irvine set a World Professional 100 yards record of 9.3 seconds at Dubbo in New South Wales. In the same year he twice registered Australian record times for 120 yards at 11.3 seconds. In his prime he was hailed as "The Fastest White Man In The World" and that included both amateur and professional sprinters.

Ken Irvine was born in Sydney, New South Wales, in 1940 and sadly passed away at the age of 50, after a long battle with leukaemia, in Brisbane, Queensland, subsequent to a career that would be the envy of any sportsman of any era. For such a great athlete his sprinting achievements have been exceptionally difficult to research and I recognize the assistance I have received from several sources in Australia.

Regarding his rugby league career much more information is available about the man who the Australians and many global pundits reckon to be the greatest winger ever to

recognition of their service and achievements. This gent certainly demonstrates a lifetime in both areas.

Born on 16th October 1936, it would appear that this athletics phenomenon didn't actually take up professional sprinting until he was around 25 years of age. His standing as a sprinter saw him at the age of almost 34 running from the back mark in the final of The Stawell Easter Gift, conceding 4 yards to eventual winner Barry Foley, who would take the win again in 1972, at which meeting Austin placed 2nd in the Bill McManus Backmarkers Handicap 440 yards.

The Tasmanian Latrobe Gift saw Reg Austin take the spoils in 1965,1966 and 1969 over 130 yards and in 1973 over 120 metres. The Wangaratta Gift fell to his pace in 1975.

As a veteran in the World Masters Championships, Reg Austin claimed the gold medals in the 1977 40-44 age group at 100 metres in 10.8 seconds and 200 metres in 21.9 seconds ; in the same age group in 1979 and 1981 he did it again over 200 metres in 22.5 and 22.53 seconds respectively. 1983 and 1985 saw him compete in the 45 to 49 age group, taking out the 100 metres in 1985 at 11.67 seconds, following victories at 200 and 400 metres in 1983 clocking 22.4 seconds and 50.61 seconds. Contesting the 50 to 54 years age group in 1987 he shared the 100 metres title with Kenny Dennis of USA, both registering 11.24 seconds, but Austin clocking 23.12 and 51.81 seconds respectively took both the 200 and 400 metres titles. That same age group saw him win the 200 metres in a windy 22.88 seconds in 1989 and follow this with a triple in 1991 over 100, 200 and 400 metres in 11.88, 23.55 and 53.63 seconds – not bad at 55 years of age!

The foregoing is just a modicum of information about the man that was good enough to provide me with the following, which is an extract of a reply on Ken Irvine's sprinting abilities, when he kindly stepped in on behalf of Australian sprint sage Jack Giddy to whom I had written re Ken Irvine :-

"...................My name is Reg Austin OAM. I have trained with Jack for 45 years a bit of a partnership. You asked about Ken Irvine, he was a good friend of mine. I remember when he broke the 100 yards professional record. I was about 3 yards back I ran second. Ken was an equally good runner as he was a footballer.......................... I also remember a Gilgandra Gift over 120metres, Irvine was off scratch................................Kenny broke and had to go back a yard, put his blocks on the concrete bike track, and still won, one of the best runs I have ever seen."

In his prime Ken Irvine was hailed as "The Fastest White Man In The World" and that included both amateur and professional sprinters. If we take 1963, when he was setting 100 and 120 yards World times, then that statement, as far as my research goes, is certainly true.

Only one sprinter Worldwide posted a faster time - "Bullet" Bob Hayes who clocked 9.1 seconds for 100 yards at The Public Schools Stadium in St Louis, USA on June 21st 1963, on a rubberised track surface specifically laid for the AAU National Track Championships he was competing in that year and, I was surprised to learn from USATF - Administrative Division - Records Committee Member for Men's Track & Field, Bob Hersh, it was a wind aided time.

As I have often argued the factor of track surface, because there is an acknowledged differential between grass, cinder and synthetic performances, can be considered seriously when comparing those 1963 performances of Ken Irvine and Bob Hayes.

Both events were hand timed, one on a grass track the other on a rubberised surface of which Hayes was noted as being full of praise.

Using the generally agreed factor of 0.25 second that a sprinter would gain from competing on a synthetic track, Ken Irvine's 9.3 reassigned from the grass track of Dubbo, NSW, to that rubberised surface in St Louis, USA, could easily have

been faster than the great Bob Hayes had run. Ken Irvine on a synthetic track 9.05 seconds - why not?

Simply converting Irvine's best at 9.3 on grass from a hand time into an electronic timing would place him in second place on the Australian All-Time List over 100 yards. The only superior Australian performance, better by just two hundredths of a second, was actually achieved in the 1966 Commonwealth Games in Jamaica on what would obviously have been an enhanced quality track surface.

Taking cognisance of all of the above it could well have been that Ken Irvine in 1963 was actually "The Fastest Man In The World".

One thing is certain.

Kenneth John Irvine is certainly an outstanding contender for the title "The Fastest Man Ever To Play Rugby League."

JOHNSTON Greville Roderick "Grev": (1909 – 1976)

Circa 6ft tall and 12 stones (1.82m / 76kg) "Grev" played 8 seasons for Barrow R.L.F.C. during the 1930s. After seeking a career initially with Barrow Association Football Club, he changed codes and became a Barrow Rugby League wingman at the age of 21. **His 65 tries scored for the first team were at the rate of basically a try in every two games played. He once registered 10 tries in an "A" team game.** "Grev" was very fast indeed as not only my father but many other "old timers" stated to me that if ever there was a man on the rugby field, in full playing kit, jersey etc, carrying the ball, in the same class as Frank Castle, the Club's international flying left wing during the 1950s it could have been "Grev" Johnston. **I have heard stories of how this "even timer" professional sprinter, given a little free space, was uncatchable and of how when partnered by a certain centre who came to Barrow from Wakefield Trinity in the form of Great Britain player one Gilbert Robinson, was often given that free space and ordered to "run, you B..., run."** Too many people have told me about "Grev" Johnston for the stories to be based upon anything other than fact and, although I never saw him play, I did see him compete as a veteran professional sprinter. I guess he would be circa 45 years old at the time and was, even then, only receiving 2 to 3 yards start in a 100 yards race from some very good young sprinters and, on watching him run, one could easily discern that Johnston must have been a class act in his younger days. **"Grev" was a very prominent pace merchant both on the rugby field and running track in the 1930s and was still sprinting in handicaps in the 1950s; he was also no mean long jumper.**

His durability as a sprinter is perhaps well illustrated by his winning double (100 and 220 yards handicaps) at Ambleside in 1951 The Lake District Ambleside Sports took place on Thursday 26th July and there were over 400 entries with the prize money increased to a record £500 (over £17000 purchasing power today) in celebration of The Festival of Britain, resulting in a record attendance of 4500 at the gate. The Men's 100 Yards and 220 Yards Handicaps finals both saw "Grev", now 43 years old, first across the finish.

"Grev" followed this by his performance at Grasmere, in the same year, where he finished in second place in the 100 yards Handicap no less than 15 years after he had placed third in the Long Jump at the same venue. In fact, he was still competing at least two years later.

The 1952 Ambleside Sports took place on Thursday 24th July, "Grev" Johnston was again expected to win the Men's 100 Yards Handicap, but with many good sprinters running off decent marks, after winning his heat and semi-final in 9.4 seconds, "Grev" had to be satisfied with 2nd place.

"Grev" Johnston – definitely a pace maestro on the pitch and on the track.

JONES Berwyn: (1940-2007)
"Flyer meets Flyer"

The athletics world was, to say the least, shocked when Jones signed for Wakefield Trinity at a fee reported to be £6,000, (purchasing power today circa £130,000) for it was Olympic year 1964 and Jones was a member of a well fancied sprint relay quartet for Britain. He had, the previous year, set a Welsh National record for the 100 metres at 10.3 seconds.

Playing under the name of "A. Walker", he had impressed in reserve team games against Huddersfield and Doncaster.

Berwyn scored 2-tries in Wakefield Trinity's 18-2 victory over Leeds in the 1964–65 Yorkshire Cup Final.

Berwyn Jones meets Tom Van Vollenhoven. By kind permission of Saints' Heritage Society Historian, Alex Service (2024) (www.saints.org)

He was selected for Great Britain in his first full season and registered two tries displaying his assets of lighting acceleration and, unexpected from what many imagined was a pure sprinter, great determination and a lack of fear. He only had a short career in the game but went on to tour Australia with the Great Britain squad and, although not figuring in Test matches, his success in the game gave clubs a renewed faith in the possibilities that track athletes may have for a conversion to Rugby League after several dismal failures with such signings prior to the Welshman.

The flyer also played for the Bradford Northern and St Helens clubs, Other Nationalities and a Commonwealth Thirteen which faced New Zealand in 1965.

Berwyn toured with Great Britain in 1966 to Australia and New Zealand but due to the excellent form of Bill Burgess and Brian Wrigglesworth he wasn't selected for the Test matches but even so registered 24 tries. With Bradford

Northern he registered a career best 26 tries in 1967-68 season then signed for Saints in 1969, but it was only a brief flirtation with the Knowsley Road club. He scored two tries before announcing his retirement, somewhat prematurely in the eyes of many observers. Berwyn passed away in Ross-on-Wye in January 2007, aged 66, after a long battle against illness.

If ever a class athlete came from the track to the Rugby field and made a resounding success of the conversion, such was the flying Welshman, Berwyn Jones at 5ft 9 inches and 11.5 stones (1.75m/73kg.)

Many could reasonably argue that he was the fastest ever.

From The Jackson column by Peter Jackson "Berwyn Jones paid the price for putting family first" - in The Rugby Paper 10th October 2018 recalling:-

"Berwyn Jones used to run like the wind, so much so that not even the so-called fastest man on Earth, Bob Hayes, could catch him. At London's White City in the summer of 1963, the Welshman famously held off the unbeaten America on the last leg of Britain's world record-breaking sprint relay win over the US. The victory, rounded off by one Jones with the help of two more, Ron and David, and Peter Radford, sprang out of the history books in Cardiff the other night with Berwyn's posthumous induction into the Welsh athletics Hall of Fame, eleven years after his death in Ross-on-Wye at the age of 66. Ironically, both he and Hayes left the track for very different codes of football."

Clive Williams of Welsh Athletics remembers:-

"The number of great Welsh track and field athletes who excelled as rugby players is greater than the mythical Max Boyce outside-half factory.

He won his first representative vest in 1960 running for the Welsh AAA against the AAA after finishing runner-up in that years Welsh Championship. He also took both Monmouthshire sprint titles that year.

But whilst Berwyn became an outstanding player of the 13-a-side game, first and foremost he was a world-class track and field athlete. His greatest claim to fame came as a member of the Anglo Welsh sprint relay team dubbed "The Jones Boys" which equalled the world 4 x 110 yards record at the White City London in 1963. The time was also a Commonwealth and European record. The fearsome foursome of Berwyn, Ron and David Jones plus the 1960 Olympic 100m bronze medallist and former Cardiff student Peter Radford beat the mighty USA with a time of 40.0 seconds at the then home of British athletics.

The USA quartet included Bob Hayes, the man destined to win the following year's Olympic 100m, who ran on the last leg against Berwyn. The Welshman said at the time: "I took over

a couple of yards up, and could feel him coming closer and closer, but I just managed to hold on."

*The time matched the world record held by the USA national team and teams from Texas and Oregon Universities. **45 days earlier Hayes had set a new world 100 yards record of 9.1 secs, equivalent to 10.0 for 100m.***

*Hayes was one of the world's all-time great sprinters, having equalled the world 100 yards record of 9.3 secs at the tender age of 18. Coupled with setting the world record of 9.1 secs and taking double gold in the 1964 Olympics at 100m (equalling the world record of 10.0 secs) along with the 4 x 100m relay (world record 39.0 secs), he rightly takes his place in the all-time great category. He went on to be a star of American Football with the Dallas Cowboys. Hayes also set world records at 60 yards (5.9 secs indoors) and 220 yards (20.6 secs) in 1963.......**our man.....showed him a clean pair of heels – such was the brilliance of Berwyn. Mel Watman in his report in Athletics Weekly said that Berwyn withstood the blistering assault of Hayes to score a victory that will be discussed for a long time to come.***

.......a tremendous track season in 1963, with no one – probably including Berwyn - expecting the startling news the following year of his move to rugby league. He took the British 100 yards title and in his best ever performance equalled the British record for 100m with 10.3 seconds in Budapest, a time that placed him in the top half-dozen in the world that year. During that signature year, he became only the second Welsh athlete to win the AAA (British) 100 yards title after Fred Cooper who had won way back in 1898.

Berwyn's best time of over half a century ago would have won him the 2014 Welsh title. In my estimation, amongst Welsh sprinters, only former world 110m hurdles record holder Colin Jackson (best of 10.29secs) and current Welsh record holder (10.11) and former world junior champion Christian Malcolm would get anywhere near him today.

In total Berwyn set eight Welsh records at either 100 yards or 100 metres and became the first Welsh athlete to clock 9.6 for 100 yards (approx.10.5 for 100m)................ Altogether, he won nine British vests, but would have won many more had he not gone North.

So over 50 years have passed since Berwyn helped to put Wales on the world sprinting map, but half a century on he would still hold his own against Britain's best. It is only now when his athletics achievements are revisited it can be appreciated how great an athlete he was.

He was inducted into the Welsh Athletics Hall of Fame in 2018. "

Incidentally,having turned "pro" Berwyn Jones is recorded has having at least one fling in the professional track scene – well nearly!

One of the main attractions, if not the foremost, at The Jedburgh Border Games in Scotland was always the Jedforest Handicap Sprint over 120 Yards. It was in 1964 that the fastest time ever recorded for the event was claimed by Bill Robertson of Lochgelly, Fife, Scotland. It was also the year that saw an entry from Berwyn Jones. The great Ricky Dunbar of Edinburgh, Scotland, who won his heat from "scratch", on a grass track, in 11.34 seconds (marginally better than 6½ yards inside "even time") testified to the standard of the event.

Berwyn was apparently to take part in the Jedforest Handicap and in a Special Invitation against Ricky Dunbar. **It is recorded that the Welsh flyer never bothered to get changed into his track gear because, after discussing terms and expenses, he decided not to run claiming what was offered was "ridiculous".** The Special Invitation was actually taken in a time almost 5 yards inside "evens" by McAnany of Blyth, Northumberland.

The great multi-talented Berwyn Jones died in January 2007
after a battle with motor neurone disease.

KILLEEN Len: (1938-2011)
Masterful South African Flyer

History has proven that South African R.U. has been a good hunting ground for the discerning League scout and one such capture was wingman Len Killeen who signed for St Helens in 1962.

Not quite as devastatingly fast as his Saints colleague Tom Van Vollenhoven on the field of play, he could still show a clean pair of heels to most and once scored a full length of the field try against Warrington.

Len was credited with a 100 yards in 9.8 seconds in 1964.

He won the Lance Todd trophy in the 1966 Challenge Cup Final against Wigan; scoring a try and five goals from five attempts. Len Killeen would score tries when the opposition least expected because he was such an unorthodox player.

A week after the Cup Final, Saints beat Halifax in the Championship Final by 35 -12. Len scored three tries and six goals!

(Many thanks are due to Alex Service and Saints Heritage Society who supported my research into Len Killeen including Len's photograph.)

He played 187 games for Saints registering 1161 points (115 tries /408 goals). **In his first season he ran in 25 tries in 27 games!**

Len Killeen is the only player ever to top the Rugby League Try - Scorers and Goal - kickers table in the same season which was 1965/66.

I once saw Len and Kel Coslett give a display of goal kicking after a league match, using a "Grid Iron" football which the coach of one of the U.S.A. leading teams had said could not be kicked for the prodigious distances that he had seen reported in newspaper articles about Killeen in particular.

Needless to say, Coslett and Killeen sent the coach back to the States with a red face and an insight to their great kicking abilities.

[On that occasion Len placed the ball on halfway at the centre spot, took one step, looked at the posts and kicked a beautiful conversion followed by a smiling effort from way out on the touchline – one step – whack - it flew over the goalposts.]

Len Killeen finished up his career in Australia with Balmain Tigers for the 1967 season and won a Grand Final Winner's medal. When he left Balmain Tigers in the early 1970s for Penrith Panthers, with whom he played eight games scoring 2 tries and 15 goals, he had scored in his 80 match career with Balmain 36 tries, and 278 goals including drop goals.

In 1969 he registered 207 points which remains a Balmain tigers record to this day. Len Killeen is a Hall of Fame Member of both Saints and Balmain clubs.

LAKE Trevor:

(Unable to establish D.O.B. or D.O.D.)

This Rhodesian flier is best remembered for his two magnificent tries in the Wigan jersey when they defeated Hunslet at Wembley to take the Challenge Cup in 1965. **Lake was their leading try - scorer of the period and was rather slim of physique for the rigours of League rugby but lacked nothing in guts.**

Looking back, Trevor was definitely underrated by many in terms of pace which he possessed in abundance and coupled with the most elusive running style which was augmented by a long striding gait, he took many confident defences by surprise for, once away, he was uncatchable.

Trevor was a Rhodesian rugby union winger who switched to rugby league and played for Wigan from 1962 to 1966. He scored 132 tries in 140 appearances for Wigan and was the top try-scorer in English club football in 1964-65 with 40 tries. He later played for Sydney St George in Australia but retired due to a knee injury.

Paraphrasing Hendrik Snyders in http://www.sarugbyleague.co.za/ he recalls:-

"Born in Umtali in Rhodesia he played rugby union at school as a wing forward. Switching to the wing brought him more success and he played for Rhodesia and the Quagga team – a South African "Barbarians" team plus trials for the Springboks just before signing a four-year contract with Wigan on a £5,000 signing on fee. He made his debut at Central Park on 3 November 1962 and scored two tries against Oldham in a 14-14 draw. Wigan skipper Eric Ashton recognised his talent:- **"He was a good finisher. You never had to look for him. If you broke, he'd be with you. He was a great talent."**

Trevor played 17 league matches in the 1962-63 season, scoring 10 more tries to add to his debut two.

1963-64 for Trevor was a brilliant season - 43 tries in 40 appearances.

In 1964-65 he played in every match on the way to Wembley, scored a try in the first round against Barrow and then got two against Swinton in the semi-final. In the final Wigan faced Hunslet, and won 20-16 in one of the greatest finals of all time. Trevor scored twice, with his second effort a swallow dive into the corner. He also topped both Wigan's and the Rugby League try scorers lists with 40 from 34 appearances.

Trevor played for a Commonwealth XIII against the New Zealand tourists at the start of the 1965-66 season. Wigan returned to Wembley for the Challenge Cup Final, this time to play local rivals, St Helens. He missed the first-round win over Halifax, but played in every other

Challenge Cup match, including a four-try haul against Whitehaven in the second round. But the final was somewhat of a disaster - Wigan lost 21-2.

Trevor scored 32 tries in the season, topping the Wigan try list, and finishing joint top with Saints Len Killeen in Rugby League try scorers lists.

With only a few weeks left on his contract, Wigan refused to pay the £3,000 Lake wanted to extend his stay with the club. He did however help Wigan in the Lancashire Cup – scoring in the first round win at Leigh.

In four years at Central Park, he scored 132 tries in 140 appearances and was the top try scorer for the club in the three full seasons he played.

He then signed for St George in Australia receiving a reputed £12,000 signing on fee. He only played eight matches in two years, scoring four tries. A knee injury in 1968 finished his career in Australia, and he returned to South Africa in 1969".

LARGE Ken: (1939 – 1995)
A Centre With Extraordinary Pace

Famous for his part in the 1961 Challenge Cup Final try, scored by Tom Van Vollenhoven, when Saints beat Wigan 12 - 6, **Ken Large was not far adrift of the great Springbok in terms of pace and his contribution to this try, which for many, was the best that Van Vollenhoven ever scored, was a major one because he was able to keep up with the flying Springbok and inter-passed with him causing the Wigan defence substantial confusion.** Ken Large had replaced the legendary Doug Greenall as centre to the illustrious all-time great wing. No superior description of this great try is better than that provided by **Saints Heritage Society -** *Dick Huddart pounced on a loose ball as a Wigan attack broke down close to the St Helens line. Stand-off Alex Murphy, who had scored the first Saints try, moved the ball wide to centre Ken Large, who beat two opponents with a sizzling burst of speed and passed to van Vollenhoven just before half way.*

Many thanks are due to Alex Service and Saints Heritage Society who supported my research into Ken Large including Ken's photograph.

The Springbok ace accelerated away from Carlton and, seeing his way blocked by Griffiths, gave a return pass inside to the supporting Large. The pair kept up their scorching pace along the touchline and two red shirted defenders raced across in a desperate effort to cover, Large whipped the ball outside to Vollenhoven once more, who streaked away to touch down between the posts after a magnificent display of controlled running and passing at speed. It was his 7th try of the cup campaign and was pure Wembley magic!

I can vouch for the above as I am proud to say, "I was there".

A product of the famous Cowley School and St Helens R.U. Club, Ken was not a big man but was one of the best centres in the game in his time and always dangerous because of his outstanding pace.

[During the period mid-1950s to mid-1960s Saints must have had more top speed merchants than any other club, perhaps in the history of the game. Names that come to mind, apart from Tom Van Vollenhoven and Ken Large, are Frank Carlton (covered in this book); Alec Davies, a champion sprinter in his youth and member of a Northern Counties Athletics Association Sprint Relay Championship winning squad for his club Earlestown Viaduct A.C.; Eric Ledger, another three quarter with extreme pace that enabled him to register 32 tries in 35 matches; Sam Clemson, a Pilkington Recs Athletics Club flyer who clocked 9.9 seconds for the 100 yards and better than "evens" also over 220 yards, except for an injury, may well have been selected for the Melbourne Olympics.]

All played first grade to a lesser or greater extent.

In his first season after signing in 1957 Ken scored 21 tries in 23 games. In 1959-60 season he scored 28 tries in 36 games.

This acknowledged true flyer played 136 matches for Saints and scored 83 tries. Transferred to Leigh RLFC for the 1962-63 season Ken played 31 times over two seasons for the club and scored 11 tries.

LEVULA Josefa (Joe): (1930 – 1989)
"The Stanley Matthews of Fiji"

Josefa (Joe) grew up in Narewa, Nadi and is remembered worldwide for his outstanding feats on the rugby field representing Fiji Rugby Union.

The Fiji Sun Sports desk 14 Mar 2013 reported that " In 1951, over 3000 fans gathered around Buckhurst Park to witness the finals between Suva and the Northern District. To the amazement of the crowd, a 21-year-old Levula scored four tries to end Suva's 10 year stranglehold on the trophy. The same year, he toured with the Fiji rugby team to New Zealand where he scored a brace of tries to help the Fiji team down the Maoris 21 – 14.

He attained New Zealand Rugby's honour that of being nominated as 'Player of the Year' The citation for this honour reads:

"Josefa Levula is indeed a great wing three-quarter; we believe the world's best"

[The legendary Jesse Owens (first black man to win the 100 metres gold medal at the Olympic Games) heard that there was a man from the Fiji Islands who ran the 100 yards in under 10 seconds. Owens wanted to meet this man and met him in Malaya. The man was none other than Flying Fijian Josefa Levula.]

Pictured in the Sydney Sun,10th August 1952 During Fiji's Spectacular Rugby Union Second Test win, 17 points to 15 against Australia, on the previous day, at the Sydney Cricket Ground before 42,004 spectators.

This fine Fijian athlete was born 1930 and I first became aware of him via a 1950 sports annual from which I remember being impressed by a photograph of this Fijian International Rugby Union player.

In full stride and carrying the ball,this giant wingman looked awesome, wearing size 11 boots and 1.94m. (6 ft 4 ins) and 105 kg (16 st.7 lbs). I thought he seemed even larger than that. Joe could play on either wing and had a reputation for 30 yard passes in Rugby Union whilst also having been reported as a capable goal kicker.

The 1950 write up said that the Fijian international was a big star in the game and with a stride reckoned to be in excess of 8ft., could run 100 yards in 9.6 seconds which time saw him regarded, in the southern hemisphere, as the fastest footballer in the World! Joe Levula was also thought to be of Olympic record class over the furlong.

Later that year, or maybe early 1951, I read an item by Eddie Waring, renowned Rugby League columnist and broadcaster, about the same player and how he (Eddie) thought he would make the grade in League.

Although several clubs were reported to be interested, including Wigan, nothing came of the interest mainly because of Levula's reported fear of being imprisoned in Fiji for showing interest in professional sport!

The Fijian Rugby Union team toured Australia with two wingers who, according to The Sydney Morning Herald of 5th July 1952, were.......... *"noted for their speed. Wingers Joe Levula and Kalivate Cavulati have each bettered evens, for 100 yards."*

Nine days later The Canberra Times of Monday 14th July (http://nla.gov.au/nla.news-article2859562) reported that *"Fijians May Be Offered Rugby Contracts For UK - Five of the touring Fijian footballers may receive offers to play 'big time' Rugby League in England, former rugby league international Ray Stehr, said this last night.................he had singled out five of the Fijians who he thought would be 'very popular' in England............... winger Joe Levula, centre George Cavalevu, five eighth Warne Salabogi, full back Tanlela Ranevue and forward Semesi Seruvatu...............................Officials with the team said that it was unlikely that the Fijian authorities would let any players leave Fiji........................ they were only able to make the present tour because a Government official Prince Ratu George Cakobau was travelling with them."*

Some lofty security measures for a rugby team! Efforts to sign this star athlete continued at a pace for some time.

On Thursday 4th September 1952 The Sydney Morning Herald reported

(http://nla.gov.au/nla.news-article18280355) yet another offer to Joe Levula – *"Star winger of the Fijian Rugby Union team in Australia this year, Josef Levula, has been offered £ 2,500 sterling for a League season in England.*

The offer also includes match bonuses, return passage and employment and educational facilities if he wants them. The name of the English club has not been disclosed.

In accordance with Fijian practice, the 21 year old Levula has referred the offer to his chiefs for their advice. *A brilliant sprinter, Levula is one of Fiji's tentative hopes for the next Empire Games and possibly the Olympics. Rugby Union circles are disturbed at the idea of losing him."*

[Note that the £2500 that the giant winger was offered to play for a season in England has a buying power of circa £80,000 today!]

Even two years later there were ongoing attempts to get Joe to change codes. He was refusing offers from both Australian and UK Rugby League clubs and his governing authorities were saying that Fiji would never allow him to turn professional. The 23 year old was looking forward to another tour of Australia with the Fijian Rugby Union team, taking part in the Australian Athletics Championships and also competing for his country in the Vancouver, Canada, Empire (Commonwealth) Games in July 1954. This latter aim was relinquished eventually as he seemed to have a preference for playing Rugby.

His intent to compete in the Australian Athletics Championships came good in February of that year when he registered a legal 9.7 seconds for the 100 yards in winning his heat and ran second to the great Hector Hogan (Australia) in the Championship final. Joe also ran 3rd in the 220 yards final.

What appeared to be security measures came to the fore again as Joe was ordered back to Fiji immediately following his track efforts in the Australian Championships.

Many years later lo and behold virtually as a veteran, I reckon 30 years of age, the giant Fijian signs for Rugby League club Rochdale Hornets in Lancashire.

The following appears by kind permission of the late **Bev Risman, President of The Rugby Football League 2010-2011** from the book **"The Rugby League Football Book (edited by Bev Risman), (Published 1962 by Stanley Paul – London)**

'The Stanley Matthews of Fiji'

"When Fijian Rugby Union star Orissi Dawai wrote to Rochdale Hornets' Chairman, Arthur Walker, in answer to an advertisement for Rugby League players in the Fiji Times, little did anyone realise just what a sensation would result................ he brought with him to this country one of the biggest names in Fijian sport. It was, of course, that loping, long-legged flyer Joe Levula whose scintillating speed has brought him wide acclaim.

Not that his supporters back home ever doubted it, for in his own country he is known as 'The Stanley Matthews of Fiji'. *He was generally acknowledged as the best in every sport he took part in. He was a top basketball player and a top sprinter as well as twice touring New Zealand with the Fijian Rugby Union team. It was in New Zealand that Joe's talents were first spotted and the news immediately flashed across the oceans to England.*

Warrington, Wigan and Workington showed interest after a bid to sign him by Sydney St. George Rugby League Club had failed due to the Australian immigration laws. But big Joe was not interested. He was quite happy with his job as a clerk. During the second New Zealand tour, however, when Orissi was captain, word reached the ears of the Hornets chairman of some fine Fijian players. Hoping Joe would be interested, Mr Walker advertised but Joe didn't respond.

Among 25 replies one was from Orissi.

Mr. Walker takes up the story: "In my advertisement I made no false promises. I made it clear that anyone wishing to come to England to join Hornets would not get a signing-on fee. I guaranteed to find them jobs and accommodation and nothing else. They were not to expect any special treatment over the rest of the players at the Athletic Ground. They would have to play for their places in the team like anybody else. I held out little hope of getting Levula because I knew he had already turned down a considerable offer to join an English club. Orissi said that if we wanted him at Rochdale, he had a cousin who was a good rugby player and who was willing to come over with him, if we were interested. Knowing Orissi's capabilities from my source in New Zealand I was delighted to get his services. I wrote back saying it would be all right for him to bring his cousin along too. Imagine my surprise when I found out that the cousin in question was Joe Levula."

Rochdale may as well be a town in Fiji, so close have the links become between them since 1961 when the club placed that advert in the Fijian press hoping to attract Rugby Union players. Fortunately Orissi Dawai, also a Fijian International winger and Joe Levula were drawn and decided to try their skills in UK, a decision which was good for Rochdale Hornets, the town of Rochdale and Rugby League in England. Certainly, Josefa Levula was to become a star attraction wherever he played, even as a veteran starting out in a completely foreign climate both in terms of weather and culture not to mention the differences between Union and League.

Between 1951 and 1961 in Rugby Union, representing Fiji, Joe played 17 games scoring 8 tries. Joe had a reputation for trying, often with success, to run over the top of opposing wingers rather than around them!

At Rochdale Hornets between 1961 and 1964 he made his first team debut on 11th November 1961 at Whitehaven and over the next three years scored 37 tries in 80 appearances before leaving in 1964 to join Bradford Northern for a fee of £1,500.

I have always thought what a great pity it was that Josefa Levula couldn't have been signed in his prime. Who knows, he may have then ranked with the very best of them all - he certainly had the size and speed.

Josefa (Joe) Levula passed away 2nd July 1989, age 59, at Rochdale.

He was inducted into the Fiji Sports Hall of Fame in 1990.

LEWTHWAITE "Gentleman" Jim: (1920 – 2006)

I remember a radio interview given by Brian Bevan to Phil King, that revered R.L. scribe, when one of the questions was who did Bevan rate as the best wingmen in the game besides himself. Bevan was actually reluctant to name anyone but offered the thought that *"if Jimmy Lewthwaite of Barrow had an extra yard, he could be the best of the lot."*

The comment by "Bev" was just an illustration of how well thought of in the game "Gentleman Jim" was and indeed he had real pace. Jim was an idol in his home town of Cleator Moor as far back as 1930 when he displayed his fleetness of foot in winning a Gold Medal and Cup at the West Seaton Miners Welfare Sports. Four years later Jim set a new record for 220 yards at Cumberland County Schools Championships which stood for over a decade. He went on collecting medals for sprinting. His ability as a track sprinter is best exemplified by the fact that he was a medallist in the All England Championships whilst at school and, believe me, to win a medal in that Championship, one really does have to have outstanding ability.

"Gentleman Jim" racing in for another try against Western Districts at Orange in N.S.W. on the 1946 Tour. (Photo supplied to me by "Gentleman Jim" Lewthwaite)

A native of Cleator Moor, Jim Lewthwaite retained an interest in athletics which had been nurtured in the Cumberland & Westmorland professional sprinting scene from a very early age.

Sprinting, Rugby Union at Junior County level, Wrestling, Soccer, any of which Jim Lewthwaite could have competed in at the highest levels, such was his all-round sporting ability. Blackburn Rovers, Wolves and Preston North End were all keen to sign this athlete who in 1936/37 season had scored a magnificent 67 goals for Barrow junior club Crystal Palace.

Events proceeded and in February 1943 Jim Lewthwaite signed for Barrow Rugby League Club beginning a 14 years 63 days career that few if any could ever match. Within a year Jim was a County player as well as topping Barrow's try scoring list. Dave Huitson, Keith Nutter and Steve Andrews summed it up most appropriately in their book "Keeping The Dream Alive" (2008), *"That he achieved greatness would be seriously understating his case. He transcended greatness both as a Rugby League player, with his adopted home town of Barrow, and, perhaps more importantly, as a person. Not for nothing was he known as "Gentleman Jim."*

One hears of players, from time to time, that have a reputation for being fair and clean but in Jim Lewthwaite's case the adjectives really did describe the club, county and international wingman. His sportsmanship was outstanding.

With a swerve and hand - off par excellence and a cross - kick timed to perfection, "Gentleman Jim" Lewthwaite had all the skills, many of which are missing in today's wingers. Defensively nothing passed Jim Lewthwaite with his ball 'n' all tackle which on many occasions, when faced with two or three attackers, saved the day for Barrow.

Jim Lewthwaite scored almost 400 tries in his career which saw him play for Cumberland County on many occasions, tour Australasia in 1946 and play at Wembley in three Challenge Cup Finals, once as a victor. Jim also had one England Cap when he played against Other Nationalities in 1952 at Huddersfield, scoring a try and, incidentally, on the other wing for England was club colleague Frank Castle.

500 appearances for Barrow RLFC -354 tries – a club record of 50 tries in his last season 1956/57 beating Frank Castle's 47 set up in 1951/52.

Great Britain top try scorer on the 1946 tour to Australasia – 25 tries – failing to score in only three matches and was the first ever G.B. tourist to score 7 tries in a single game!

Regarding his pace, Jim told me that he felt he was better over the 220 yards than he was over the 100 and I know of two dreadful injuries that he endured with, shall we say, less than adequate treatment being administered at the time, one on the 1946 Tour and one two years later sustained against Oldham, both to the same part of his physique.

I first saw Jim play in the late 1940s and came into contact with him over the years for several varying reasons. When I was researching my book *They Could Catch Pigeons* he threw in his help and thoughts quite freely. Perhaps I can illustrate just a little more about this fine athlete by the following :-

Below is a transcript of a letter "Gentleman Jim" Lewthwaite penned to me after the publication of *They Could Catch Pigeons* in 1996 which gives the reader further insight to this fine athlete's pace.

Barrow in Furness.

Dear Ray,

Many thanks for the copy of your book.

I must congratulate you and any helpers you had on the tremendous amount of research you would have to undertake in the compiling of this book. You picked on a very debateable subject as to the timing of players as you quite rightly remark, were they timed on a running track as a sprinter or on the field in full Rugby gear carrying a ball?

Conditions on sports stadiums, starting blocks etc has enhanced sprinting times, the same goes for rugby grounds and players equipment plus the more intensive training carried out these days.

However, my reason is more of a personal one for this letter and it is the question of injuries. When I was selected for and went on the 1946 Tour I was just about the fastest winger in the game. I was quite a raw recruit to Rugby and speed was my main asset.

In my first game in Australia I was trampled on and received severe contusions to my left calf muscle.Being continually on the move as touring teams had to be I was unable to receive the intensive treatment required so it cost me a yard or two in pace.

Two years later playing against Oldham I received a kick whilst playing the ball from the second row forward called Tomlinson. I limped through the last 20 minutes of the game and as I was standing in the shower I could see my leg beginning to swell (the left calf muscle). The following morning, Sunday, after a very restless night, my leg from the tip of my toes to my groin had swollen to twice its size and was every colour from brown, blue, black, you name it.

I had not received any medical attention whatsoever, so on the Monday I saw the Club Doctor at the Hospital who calmly told me the kick had burst a vein in my leg.

It was six weeks before I could place my left foot on the ground. The injury cost me 8 matches and goodness knows how many yards off my speed. In all my career it was the worst injury I had to bear, the pain was terrific.

I only tell you this to prove how difficult it is to assess the speed of Rugby Players.

Thank you once again for some very enjoyable reading.

Yours in Sprinting,

Jim Lewthwaite.

"Gentleman Jim" Lewthwaite - what an athlete, what a true gentleman.

At around the 6ft mark and 13 stone plus, "Gentleman Jim" could and did score from anywhere on the ground, 2 yards out, 20 yards, 70 yards, it didn't really matter for once into his ground - eating stride he was as unstoppable as any Boston, Cooper or Tuigamala and faster!

With "Gentleman Jim" on one wing and Frank Castle on the other, Barrow in the '50s, had devastation to unleash.

MANTLE John: (1942 – 2018)
Multi-talented Athlete

(Many thanks are due to Alex Service and Saints Heritage Society who supported my research into John Mantle including John's photograph.)

In Rugby Union John played for Bargoed RUFC, Loughborough Colleges and Newport RUFC. It was from the latter, where he won two Welsh caps, that this massively built athlete, widely talented in several sports signed for St Helens in 1965 in spite of considerable interest from Wigan.

Well over 6ft (1.83 m.) and circa 15 stones(95.3 kg.) he is recognized as one of the fastest forwards ever to play the game and certainly for Saints.

In key Rugby League historian Robert Gate's words *"John Mantle took to the game like a duck to water…."* and merged seamlessly into a Saints pack that included such as Bob Dagnall, Ray French, Mervyn Hicks Doug Laughton. John Tembey, John Warlow, Cliff Watson et al.

In a stellar career in Rugby League where he could perform equally well in the backs or forwards John registered,between 1965 and 1982, 554 club games and 75 tries. Of those, 435 games and 69 tries were with Saints. He also played for Salford, Leigh, Barrow, Keighley, Oldham, Blackpool Borough and Cardiff Blue Dragons.

Winning every honour in the game, with Saints his record reveals:-

League Championships in 1965-66, 1969-70, 1970-71, 1974-75;

Challenge Cup 1966, 1972, 1976;

League Premiership 1976;

Lancashire Cup 1967-68;

Lancashire League 1964-65, 1965-66, 1966-67, 1968-69;

League Leaders 1964-65, 1965-66.

For Great Britain John Mantle made 13 Test appearances between 1966 and 1973; plus in tour games for Great Britain, 7 appearances.

For Wales in 1975, 13 appearances and 2 tries;

John was inducted into the St Helens Hall of Fame.

It was thought almost impossible for a club to seek a replacement for a player of the standing of Dick Huddart with any real hope of immediate success, but Saints did the trick with the signing of the Welsh giant. Not only had they signed a player of almost equal physique but also with the same kind of impressive pace! In my opinion, not quite as fast as Huddart.

John Mantle has no superior amongst today's forwards for uninhibited pace.

[As an aside I would love to have seen a race in full rugby gear between Dick Huddart, John Mantle and Jack Grundy. I believe the former Saint and Barrow second row may just have surprised both Mantle and Huddart!]

MARKHAM Ray: (1909 – 1988)
"The Australian Hare"

Ray Markham was another Aussie wingman whom the Huddersfield club seemed to have a liking for. (In the 1920 s they had signed several.) Ray came from the Cessnock Club in the Hunter Valley Region of New South Wales.

He was with Huddersfield from 1933 and registered 255 tries in his six seasons with the club.

At 12stone 2lbs (77kg) Ray stood at just under 5ft 10 inches.(1.78m).

He proved a great success for the Fartown outfit. He also won a Professional Sprint for both Rugby and Association footballers, organised at Headingley in 1933. Ray was a fine sprinter. He was always regarded as one of the fastest men in Australian Rugby League.

The Illawarra Mercury (Wollongong, NSW) Friday 29th Jul 1932 reported on

The Cessnock Eagle and South Maitland Recorder (NSW Tuesday 26th July 1932 Photo by Galloway Studios

"The Australian Hare's" win to settle an argument as to who was the fastest runner playing Rugby League football on Australia's Northern Coalfields.

S. Donegan, (formerly of Balmain) raced Ray (Wollongong). over a distance of 100 yards. They wore football boots and jerseys. Ray Markham won by 2.5 yards.

After his arrival in England the Maitland Daily Mercury (NSW) 1933 reported that:- **Ray was the "Fastest Footballer" in Britain** and took the title over 100 yards in 10.3 seconds gaining him £50 and a Gold medal. [It was unknown as to whether the race was in spikes, rugby boots, on a field or on a track.]

He also competed in the world's professional running championships at Hackney Wick Stadium, London.

Ray's success in English Rugby League was told by **A. N. Gaulton in the Rugby League journal, 'Rugby League Review',** under the heading ^Memories of Ray Markham", some of which is paraphrased here:- ....

Ray Markham was just a name to Huddersfield supporters when he was signed ....and they eagerly anticipated seeing its owner in the flesh. He arrived in time to play against Leeds and the already well established Eric Harris, early in January, 1933, and within the space of a few months was in the forefront of the many fine wingmen of the day. In that first part season Markham won a Rugby League Challenge Cup medal in the Huddersfield-Warrington final of 1933....................A clean handler and an elusive runner, Markham allied a subtle swerve to his great speed.............

Many great tries and scoring feats stand against Markham's name, it is impossible to do justice to them all.

Numerically his nine tries against Featherstone Rovers at Fartown on September 21st, 1935, must come first, yet this was an unusual rather than a brilliant feat. Nine tries are certainly a big haul for one man in one game, even allowing for the fact that there was an obvious tendency to - **'Give it to Ray'** *on the part of his colleagues...................Those who saw his three sparkling tries in the 1938 Yorkshire Challenge Cup Final against Hull at Odsal Stadium will probably award the palm to that display as Markham's best for Huddersfield. His second try was in the 'super' class. Receiving the ball just inside the Hull half, he appeared to have no chance of scoring. Once he was brought to the ground but was; up and away again before his opponents could make the tackle. Twisting and turning in and out he weaved his way through the defence and when he dived over for the touchdown there were three beaten Hull defenders stretched out on the ground behind him..........In addition to his nine tries in one game for Huddersfield, Ray scored six tries on two occasions, five once, and four seven times. In fourteen other games he finished up with three tries. With only thirteen matches played: during season 1935-36, he was a good way ahead in the scoring lists with thirty tries to his name. He finished the season as leading try scorer for the whole Rugby League, a feat repeated in 1938-39 when he graced our great game for the last time.*

A Dominion XIII rugby league team played international fixtures against France during the 1930s, the team consisted of English based non-British rugby league footballers from the dominions of the British Empire, e.g. Australia, and New Zealand. Ray was among that group and played for the Dominion X111.

During the period there was Dominion XIII's 5–8 defeat by France during the 1935–36 season at Stade Buffalo, Paris, on Sunday 26 April 1936, in front of a crowd of 12,000, and the 6–3 victory over France during the 1936–37 season at Stadium Municipal, Toulouse, on Sunday 21 March 1937, in front of a crowd of 16,000.

Australian Hares accelerate to high speed, break cover and sprint away.

So could Ray Markham

McCARTEN Ralph: (1929 - 2005)

Ralph, considered by some as a pure sprinter, had gained an Amateur International selection and played more Rugby League than he was given credit for.

A Workington Town player from 1950 - 59, this true flyer must be in the frame for fastest ever to play the game.

He first played rugby league in 1949 as an amateur for Seaton in Cumberland before signing for Workington Town in 1950, playing his first game in their reserves, still an amateur, against Wigan reserves and actually scoring a try.

Ralph had played at amateur International level - chosen for England against France.

In 1952 Workington Town played at Wembley Stadium and won the Rugby League Challenge Cup but having been a scorer of several tries in previous rounds Ralph, highly disappointed, was left out of the Final team. Rugby was actually in the family as his relative Ronald played Rugby Union for Ireland.

(Supplied by Ralph -1996)

I saw Ralph run one of the most fantastic 100 yards handicaps at Kendal Gala on Tuesday, August 4th. 1953. The big prize of the day was £15 (circa £450 in purchasing power today) for the winner of the Men's 100 Yards Handicap which attracted no less than 8 heats from 52 sprinters.

On a rain soaked grass track, (It rained all day) R. Patterson, the name Ralph McCarten ran under, was back marker, giving established and accepted good sprinters such as Tommy Trelore of Barrow 6 yards start. Through false starting Ralph ended up one yard behind scratch before the race got under way but he went on to win the event in 9.9 seconds, actually covering 101 yards and providing for all present an abiding memory of a great sprinter.

[You can take it from me that Ralph McCarten's 100 yards equivalent time (9.8) that day was possibly worth up to one fifth of a second better than was clocked. The rain, all day, and track had to be seen to be believed. I competed on it that day. On

a synthetic track (non-existent in those days) his time would have been worth 9.55 seconds.

Now then, consider that in 1953 the AAA Championship 100 Yards was won by, one of the all-time greats, Emmanuel McDonald Bailey in 9.8 seconds ; in 1954 the Championship was taken by George Ellis, actually from Keswick in Cumberland in 9.9 seconds ; 1955 saw Roy Sandstrom through in 10 seconds dead ; 1956 found the prodigious John Young claim the Championship in 9.9 seconds ; Liverpool's Ken Box clocked 10 seconds in his 1957 win ; James Omagbemi of Nigeria made a 9.9 win in 1958 and the great Peter Radford clocked a windy 9.7 seconds to take the Championship Gold Medal in 1959. All of these times were clocked on the cinder track at London's famous White City Stadium, the then home of English athletics.

So just how good was this 24 year old young athlete from Cumberland ?

The above answers that question admirably I would suggest.]

Ralph ran and won all over the professional circuit in England and Scotland at distances ranging from 100 yards to 440 yards and was credited with 3 yards inside "even time" for the short sprint.

The 1953 Centenary Jedburgh Border Games, where Ralph competed in the World famous Jedforest Handicap Sprint, over 120 yards for a first prize of £150 (circa £4,500 purchasing power today) and a gold medal, was another occasion where the Cumberland Rugby League wing flyer demonstrated his class. With the event attracting a record entry of 178 athletes, including 60 from England, although unable to win the final running off a mark of 5 yards, in his cross-tie Ralph clocked 11.18 seconds, better than 3 yards inside "even time".

Circa thirty years ago Ralph recalled for me that his - *first Big Handicap win was for the Tom Mitchell Cup at The British Legion Sports on Lonsdale Park in 1949. The next ten years were spent running and winning at meetings all over Cumberland and The Borders at 100 yards and 220 yards with the occasional 440 yards.*

Other memorable events were winning the Highland Games at Braemar and Aboyne, beating the current British Champion in both the "scratch" races and the short limit handicaps. His time at Braemar 9.8 seconds for the "scratch" race.

Competing in a 220 yards race at Keswick and clocking 22 seconds. The race was run without lanes so the back marker has to run on the outside of the other competitors.

(Ralph related that he actually went round the final bend into the finishing straight in the lead. The next thing he knew a leading international sprinter was in front of him after cutting inside the flags. Ralph didn't protest, as he did not see what had happened.)

Winning 100 yards handicaps, back to back, at Innerleithen in Scotland and Egremont in Cumberland and preceding that, 3 days earlier, with a 220 yards win at Grasmere.

Winning 100 yards and 440 yards at Cleator Moor within 2 minutes of each other.

Beating Wally McArthur to win the Penrith 100 Yards.

Ralph said his biggest disappointment was tearing his hamstring 10 yards from the tape when leading 1948 Olympian Norbert "Barney" Ewell of USA in the Keswick sprint.

(Barney Ewell had equalled the World 100 Metres Record of 10.2 seconds at the USA Olympic Trials, then at the Olympic Games in London, Ewell took the Silver medal in the 100 Metres and 200 Metres plus Gold in the 4 x 100 Metres Relay. **Such was the eminence of sprinter to whom Ralph McCarten was comparable.**)

Workington Rugby League flyer, Ralph McCarten, was certainly as good as any sprinter in the U.K. of that period. He had just one drawback that kept him from being recognised as one of the very best sprinters in Great Britain in his prime and being selected to represent his country, the fact that he chose to run as a professional!

A certain George McNeill, who also trialled at Rugby League, of a later generation, would suffer the same fate.

After his career was over Ralph spent many years coaching young athletes

McARTHUR Wally: (1933-2015)
The Borroloola Flash

(stfrancishouse.com.au)

Wally McArthur was an Aboriginal Australian rugby league winger and track and field athlete. **In 2008, the Centenary of Rugby League in Australia, he was named in the Aboriginal Australian Rugby League Team Of The Century. He was variously known as The Borroloola Flash – The Black Flash – Waltzing McArthur.**

The Northern Territory of Australia has running through it a McArthur River, on it the small town of Borroloola and in the relatively close vicinity within about 40 miles is the McArthur River Mining Company's McArthur River Mine and neighbouring Merlin Diamond Mine.

Silver, lead, zinc, diamonds all within the scope of the operators of such enterprises, but one nigh forgotten but sporting gem originating from the Borroloola area was the aboriginal athlete Wally McArthur. **If he was named after the area in which he was born in 1933, I am unaware, but this man was certainly a superb natural athlete if ever I saw one ; contrary to some of the stories I have heard about his ability as a sprinter, in my opinion in his day – the late 1940s to the late 1950s – he was World class.**

An exceptionally talented young athlete both at sprinting and Rugby League in New South Wales (Australia), he was credited with a 52 seconds 440 yards run at the age of 14 and Wally, after some eye opening and officially noted efforts which saw him talked up as the greatest prospect Australia possessed as a future Olympian, found himself in Adelaide (South Australia) at the age of 15. **He continued to play Rugby League, collecting an admirable assortment of successful try scoring opportunities and goal kicks with his club Semaphore and also was selected to represent South Australia.**

On Saturday, December 2nd, 1950, representing his amateur athletic club – Port Adelaide – as a 17 year old novice, the young flyer claimed a win in a Novices 75 Yards Handicap off a mark of 1½ yards untroubled in 8 seconds. He later

contested the Open 75 Yards Handicap off 5 yards and won in 7.4 seconds.

Just two weeks had passed when the young sprinter claimed another victory at St Peter's College, Adelaide in the 100 Yards Handicap. Running off a mark of 4 yards he clocked 9.9 seconds for the win.

In 1950 McArthur was still producing the goods on the Rugby field for his Semaphore club, scoring 31 points out of a total of 49 in one game against Port Adelaide, with his 5 tries and 8 goals.

He was voted South Australia's Best and Fairest Player whilst with Semaphore for which club it is reported he scored over 900 points.

Early in 1951 Wally McArthur was being talked up as a possible State Junior Sprint Champion after he had won an inter-club 100 yards race in 10.3 seconds on cinders. Later in March that year he clocked 10.5 seconds in winning a Junior sprint organised under the auspices of South Australia Amateur Athletic Association.

Melinda Andrews of Athletics South Australia informed me that Wally did indeed win a South Australia Junior 100 Yards Championship in 1951 clocking 10.5 seconds and further enlightened me regarding his athletic ability as recorded in "Athletics S.A. - A Centennial Chronicle 1905 – 2005" by Fletcher McEwen. It is argued that on 3rd February 1951 in the Senior Men's State Selection Trials held at Wayville Showgrounds, Adelaide, Scotchy Gordon beat Wally by ½ yard in the 100 Yards, clocking 10.4 seconds. Then on 10th February, Wally came 3rd behind Gordon and Bob Hehir in the 220 Yards trial, with Gordon defeating McArthur by at least the 3 yards that separated 1st and 2nd places anyway. These performances were reasoned as being an illustration that Wally McArthur's abilities were "exaggerated projections". It was further reasoned that the fact that he was an Aborigine had nothing do with the fact he was left out of the State athletics team. On those performances, the argument is difficult to oppose.

The following year – the year of the Helsinki Olympic Games - McArthur was hovering around even time with a second place off a mark of 2 yards on cinder track in Adelaide on 12th February.

Australia announced its largest ever Olympic Team, up to that point in time, for the Helsinki Games in Finland, which would run between 19th July and 3rd August 1952. As far as male sprinters were concerned the selectors chose M. J. Curotta, K. J. Doubleday, J. P. Treloar and E. W. Carr. **There was, and has been ever since, some discussion as to Wally McArthur's omission from this Olympic Squad.**

Let's have a look in some detail at those actually chosen over Wally McArthur:-

Morris Curotta from Sydney was 23 years old and had represented Australia at the 1948 London Olympic Games at 100 metres and 400 metres plus the sprint relay. The best performance I can find for him is at International level and is 10.7 seconds for 100 metres.

K. J. (Ken) Doubleday was 26 year old State of Victoria athlete entered in the 110 metres and 400 metres hurdles, who was also allocated a sprint relay place. He appears to have registered no notable personal best performances at National or International level in either of the sprint events.

John Treloar, who was about 4 to 5 years older than Wally, was considered one of the fastest sprinters in the World in the late 1940s into the early 1950s, certainly in the Commonwealth to which his double gold medals in the 100 yards/9.7 seconds and 220 yards/21.5 seconds testified. Treloar was a multiple Australian Championship winner during his career and clocked 10.76 seconds in the 100 Metres at Helsinki in his semi-final before finishing last in the final. He would appear to have legal personal best performances in National or International class competition of 9.6 second/100 yards ; 10.5 seconds/100 metres when aged 20 and a 20.9 seconds/220 yards.

E. W.(Edwin) Carr another 23 year old sprinter who had been selected to represent his country at 200 metres, 400 metres and the sprint relay. I can only find a 21.8 seconds for 200 metres registered actually at the Helsinki Games.

In the Australian Open Track and Field Championships regarding the above selected sprinters I found that :-

In the 1951-52 Championships individual events, which must surely have reflected on selections for Helsinki, Treloar was the only entry in the sprints in which he took 2nd place in the short sprint at 9.7 seconds and 1st in the furlong at 21.5 seconds. Edwin Carr won the 440 yards. Doubleday did run in the sprint relay.

In the 1950-51 Championships individual events, again Treloar the lone sprinter clocking 9.8 seconds for 2nd place and 21.8 seconds in his 220 yards heat ; going on to finish 5th in the final.

I would have thought that realistically the above two National Championships were the only ones that should have influenced selectors and, perhaps, previous showing by Treloar and Carr, the former at National and International level and the latter at National level.

Tuesday 24th March 1953 saw the Wally McArthur the Aborigine flyer make his professional sprinting debut with a win over 100 yards at Adelaide's Goodwood Oval track.

Early April that year and Wally was, in my opinion, beginning to show the promise that he had displayed as an amateur when, at Adelaide's Norwood Oval, he won £10 and the final of 75 Yards Handicap in 7.4 seconds off 4.75 yards and was a heat winner in the Metropolitan Athletic Club's 130 Yards Easter Gift off 7.5 yards in the time of 12 seconds dead. **The latter effort being better than 2 yards inside "even time" on a track in poor condition.**

North of Adelaide by some 200 miles, the 1953 Quorn Gift (South Australia), on Sat 2nd May 1953, was the scenario for Wally to win the 100 Yards All Comers in 9.6 seconds off 6 yards ; he ran second in the 75 yards event and then took out the 130 Yards Back Markers' Handicap off 5.25 yards in 12.6 seconds for the £20 prize money, 0.1 second outside "even time."

30th May 1953 saw Wally declared as Rugby League 100 Yards Champion at Adelaide's Alberton Oval during a contest involving inter- state rugby league squads.

The following extract is quoted, by kind permission of Margaret Cazabon, Parliamentary Web Manager, Department of Parliamentary Services, Parliament House, Canberra ACT 2600, Australia, related to a publication I completed in 2012.

"Documentary on Aboriginal Living Conditions ; Panel Discussion

28th Sept. 1999"

Wally McArthur recalls: *"I went in the 100 yards, the 440 yards and the long jump - you know, the broad jump. We called it broad jumping in them days. And I found out later that I won the three out of three. I was the only one in the school history up till that time to win three out of three. And I ran barefoot and I saw in the paper the next day that it was the fastest 440 yards for a 14-year-old in the World... The professional body came up to me and they said: "Look, we'll look after you if you turn pro", and they did look after me really good before I went to England. **The first 10 races I ran as a pro, I won - 10 of them. One of them was against Frank Banner. He was an Australian professional sprint champion. They flew him from Sydney here to Adelaide. I ran against him at one of the football ovals there, Norwood Oval, and he gave me a four-yard start. I beat him by six; I ran away from him.**...................................*

*When I arrived there (England) I wasn't looking for recognition or anything like that, but I got the paper next day, you know, and there was a photo on the front page and it had the headlines: **"Black flash on way to England"**. And I thought: eh, gee whiz. I looked at my skin, you know, and said I'm not that black, am I, surely? But anyway, that was in London, in the London Times, and I got on the train and went up to Manchester. The cameras were there waiting when I got off the train and photo on the front page of the Manchester News, and it had: **coffee-coloured boy from South Australia arrives in Manchester**. I thought gee whiz, I'm black in one paper and coffee coloured in the other one.*

When I was a professional in England I won the Northern England 100 yards and 220 yards, and that same day the Empire Games were being held at Cardiff in Wales, and my times of the 100 and 220 yards were far superior to the Australian runners representing Australia at that time................ "

Did Wally McArthur ever beat Frank Banner the Australian Professional Sprint Champion ?

Well to answer this let me take you via the following news item **W.A. Coach Voices His Confidence. (1953, July 30). The West Australian (Perth, WA :**

1879-1954),p.14.Retrieved March 16 2011 from http://nla.gov.au/nla. news-article49223582 :-

"W.A. Coach Voices His Confidence:

Western Australia will make a great bid for victory when it plays South Australia at Higham Park on Sunday in the first interstate rugby league match to be held in Perth since 1948.

R. Chester, coach of the West Australian team which won the southern States carnival in Adelaide recently, said yesterday that he was confident the side would beat South Australia. "The key to our success lies in the ability of Robson to win most of the scrums." he said. Chester added: "The all-round pace of our three-quarters should enable W.A. to score more tries than South Australia. "The former St. George player, Jack Fitzgerald, together with the other centres Plester and Thompson, who played so well in Adelaide, will greatly strengthen our attack".

Quoting 'Outpaced' "However, South Australia has the fastest footballer I have ever seen. He is Wally McArthur, a winger, who several times in Adelaide easily outpaced our speediest players." McArthur is South Australia's fastest professional sprinter. He recently beat the Australian professional sprint champion, Frank Banner, over 130 yds, when receiving only a 2 yd. Start. Several first grade Sydney clubs are negotiating for his services, but McArthur is reluctant to leave Adelaide................"

How good was Banner at that period of his career ? Well you decide after reading the following :-

BANNER NOW LEADS PRO. RUNNERS. (1953, March 23). The Argus (Melbourne, Vic. : 1848-1954), p. 10. Retrieved March 18, 2011, from http://nla.gov.au/nla.news-article23234964

"When Frank Banner won the Australian professional sprint title at Lilydale on Saturday, he completed a brilliant comeback after two disappointing seasons.

He has now regained top ranking in Australian professional running.

Victory in the 130 yards championship event gave him a clear cut win in the series of four races.

Banner, who previously had held the Australian crown in 1948, finished this year's series with a total of 17 points.

This gave him an advantage of six points over Victorian Norm McDonald. Gerald Hutchinson, also of Victoria, was third, and Queenslander Ken Trewick fourth.

Banner, who had announced he would retire if not successful in the championships, won three of the four events contested.

Before his victory on Saturday he captured the 220 and 75 yards titles.

He also was placed second in the 100 yards, won by Essendon footballer Norm McDonald.

Banner led from the start in the 130 yards on Saturday, to win by a yard from McDonald in 12.4sec - six yards inside even time.

Running confidently, he was never in danger after the half-way mark.

McDonald, who lost some ground early, was in third place 20 yards from the finish. However, his final effort enabled him to defeat Hutchinson by about three inches.

Trewick finished two yards further behind in fourth place."

Therefore my comment on the foregoing is that you don't beat a National Sprint Champion, certainly one who was recently running 6 yards inside "even time", even he did give you 2 yards start over the classic 130 yards, unless you can run very fast indeed!

Wally McArthur was definitely very fast.

During all of this time of course the flying winger had been recognised, not just in Australia, as a prolific try and goal scorer at his chosen game of Rugby League.

In November a move was made by Wally to secure his future as indicated below:-

Rugby Player's Big Contract. (1953, November 13). The Advertiser (Adelaide, SA: 1931-1954), p. 10. Retrieved March 14, 2011, from http://nla.gov.au/nla.news-article48937028

"Outstanding SA and Semaphore rugby league winger Wally McArthur, a part-aborigine, has accepted a £1,000 (£30,000 purchasing power today) four year contract to play with Rochdale Hornets, a leading club in England. He will leave soon by plane. On arrival he will be paid £250 and the remaining £750 will be paid at the rate of £250 in the other three years. Rochdale Hornets will pay his plane fare and his ship fare home. The contract provides for a renewal for a further four years. In first grade in England he will be paid £8 for a win, £6 for a draw and £4 for a loss. In reserve grade he would receive £6, £4 and £2. McArthur, who is 20, is the first SA rugby league player to have received an offer from an English club. He was a promising amateur sprinter before turning professional."

A week later the same publication reported :-

Tribute To S.A, Rugby Player. (1953, November 21). The Advertiser (Adelaide, SA: 1931-1954), p. 17. Retrieved March 14, 2011, from http://nla.gov.au/nla.news-article48929886

CANBERRA. Nov 20

"Mr. Bate (Lab. NSW) asked the Prime Minister in the House of Representatives today about an Australian of part aboriginal blood who, he said, had secured a contract to play football with an English club. Mr. Bate said the young man was taken to Mulgoa as a war orphan and the Church of England, assisted by the Government, was responsible for his training. "In view of the credit he brings upon people of his blood, can the Government take an interest in him?" Mr. Bate asked. Mr. Menzies said he would take note of the information and would consider it. [The player referred to by Mr. Bate is Wally McArthur, 19, of S.A., who left Sydney on Thursday to play with Rochdale Hornets in the Lancashire Rugby League.]"

November 19th saw Wally leave Sydney and Saturday 12th December that year found McArthur making a very impressive debut for Rochdale

Hornets, before their largest crowd of the season and, apart from some exciting running with the ball, he also kicked 3 goals. This flying machine soon proved to be a crowd puller and not just because of his undoubted pace which, incidentally, had certainly been reported in the Australian press as 9.7 seconds for 100 yards.

He still created interest on running tracks, none more than at Scotland's Jedburgh Border Games where in 1954 he appeared to have been too severely handicapped to perform up to his best. The British Champion and legend of professional sprinting Albert Grant of Blyth, Northumberland, running at that period better than 4 yards inside "even time" was competing under the nom-de-plume Walter Spence and was receiving 1½ yards start from the Australian flyer in the Jedforest Handicap Sprint over 120 yards – asking a bit too much of any sprinter I reckon. McArthur did finish 3rd in the 100 Yards "Scratch" event, Grant (Spence) placing 1st and R.Patterson (nom-de-plume for Ralph McCarten) of Workington R.L. Club taking 2nd spot. Ralph McCarten was another really great sprinter from Cumberland as it was then (Cumbria now), so Wally was in superb company that day.

I was told that in 1954 Wally McArthur had taken part at an English Lake District Sports meeting in the 220 Yards Handicap. There were no lanes. In the pro sprints around a bend the first to the bend had to be overtaken and so on ; the back marker had to pass everyone else. The Australian was running from "scratch" and placed 1st in the final. However, this particular event saw a shambles at the finish with complaints being registered in which McArthur was involved and which resulted in a re-run. In the re-run he saw fit to avoid all possible contact with the other competitors and took a wide berth some 3 to 4 yards adrift of the rest, which action, of course, caused him to run well in excess of 220yards. **Needless to say, he won the race and in a time of 21.8 seconds. Some performance considering the not very good grass track, the re-run and the fact that he ran well in excess of the actual race distance.**

The following year at least the Australian may have felt more at home with the weather conditions at the Jedburgh Border Games and the fact that, instead of conceding, he was receiving ½ yard from Albert Grant (Walter Spence), who was off "scratch", in the 100 Yards Invitation Handicap event. But even that advantage was not enough for McArthur to stop the Blyth sprinter from winning.

I believe I have more than a good personal impression of how fast Wally McArthur really was. You see in the 1950s he came into English Rugby League when there were many very fast men and I was familiar with many of their respective careers and abilities on the rugby field and on the track.

Salford, Rochdale Hornets, Blackpool Borough and Workington Town were clubs that Australian flyer Wally McArthur represented, in a somewhat chequered career in League in England. McArthur played a total of 165 games on the wing with

Rochdale, Blackpool, Salford and Workington Town. He scored a total of 611 points during this time.

(I have very good reason to remember Wally McArthur for, the week after Salford RLFC transferred him, I played a trial for them and had made headlines in the Eddie Waring column in The Sunday Pictorial as the man who Salford were going to spend the money on that they had received from the transfer deal. It goes without saying that after the game the late rugby league legend Augustus John Risman, who was the coach in charge at the club, very politely told me to " think about coming back next year!")

Wally McArthur was a beautifully balanced athlete who ran with such ease that one did not realise just how fast he was moving. Poetry in motion as they say. Like many great sprinters, he made it look as though it was no effort at all. He was elusive, could tackle and had a deceptive change of pace. Not a prolific try scorer in England, he was seen in the summer months at Lakeland and Scottish professional sports meetings where he had some success. It is still debateable whether or not he was a 1952 Australian Olympic prospect with a time of 9.7 seconds for 100 yards, which I have stated above was documented in the Australian press.

It would appear that Wally McArthur, even after being in England for five years still felt he had grounds to regret that the Australian athletics authorities had never chosen him to represent his country.

He is reported to have emphasised this long standing feeling in the fact that he ran faster times over the 100 yards and 440 yards distances in England than his countrymen could achieve in the 1958 Commonwealth Games at Cardiff in Wales.

This is worth a further look, at least as far as the Australian sprinters' performances in those Games are concerned.

There were three competitors in the 100 Yards representing Australia - the great Hector Hogan, James McCann and Terence Charles Gale.

The latter went out of the competition having clocked 10 seconds, McCann went out on 10.2 seconds and even Hogan never reached the final being eliminated at the semi-final stage on 9.7 seconds.

Gale was eliminated, as the sole Australian in the 220 Yards, on a clocking of 22.1 seconds whilst Richard Kevan Gosper also found himself eliminated in the 440 Yards semi-final on 48.1 seconds.

Had I been Wally McArthur, I would certainly have felt I had strong grounds to feel the way he did especially when you look at the 100 and 220 yards performances.

Personally, I would certainly rate him amongst the fastest ever to play Rugby League anywhere ; he was actually named in the Indigenous Team Of The Century.

I believe from what I saw of this superb Aboriginal athlete, in the right circumstances at his best, he would certainly not have been out of place with John Treloar.

He proved that against the likes of Frank Banner in Australia and Albert Grant in England in my opinion.

Wally McArthur - The Borroloola Flash - fantastic athlete - like a cheetah so graceful and relaxed.

McCORMICK Stan: (1923-1999)
"The Interception Master"

One of the very best wing three quarters I ever had the privilege to see. In one of the most prolific periods for class wingers - the 1950s, Belle Vue Rangers, St Helens, Warrington, Liverpool City all saw service from this great wing "character". At a compact 5ft. 8ins. and 12 stone plus, a consistent try - scorer with all the tools of the trade and then some! Anyone who didn't know of his prowess as a professional sprinter would soon find out for he didn't need a yard from anyone. Indeed, Ray French (Saints Hall of Fame, BBC Commentator and Author) told me of the sprinting feat of which Stan was immensely proud, that of his defeating British Professional Sprint Champion W. Spence (Real name Albert Grant) in a handicap race. O.K., Stan was receiving a start but remember Spence was winner of the 1947 Powderhall Sprint and placed in the first three in 1948 and 1949, a year in which he also contested the World Professional Sprint Championship. Stan McCormick was an all action runner, using the not inconsiderable power he possessed to produce excellent acceleration

The Superb Stan McCormick

(Many thanks are due to Alex Service and Saints Heritage Society who supported my research into Stan McCormick including Stan's photograph.)

from a virtual standstill. Having witnessed his pace I would reckon that Stan was, in his prime, just inside "even time" over 100 yards and, as previously mentioned he had to his credit a defeat of the great Walter Spence (Albert Grant) in a handicap event.

Stan, in my opinion was a better than "even time" runner and was another who seemed to be able to master different ground conditions, certainly on a rugby field

and with that in mind I would venture the opinion that given a decent mark, say 5 to 6 yards, on the Powderhall cinders over the 130 yards distance against the finalists in 1949, the World Champion to be, Walter Spence may have found he was chasing another, singularly talented, athlete to the finish.

Stan was so alert to the game and what was going on around him that he was so very dangerous even without the ball, as many an opposing centre found out having made what would appear to be a scoring pass only to find McCormick had intercepted and scored himself. To Stan McCormick **"The Interception Master"** this was a common occurrence and his expertise in the art found him touching down on no less than sixteen occasions in one season from such skill.

Stan McCormick was one of those players who could certainly turn a dour game into a classic. **In the days when such as Brian Bevan and Lionel Cooper were renowned for increases in gates wherever they played, Stan McCormick will have put a few on himself for he was a spectator's dream and brought out that anticipation in the crowd whenever he was on the park.**

Stan was a Lancashire, England, born winger who represented Lancashire County, England and Great Britain at the highest levels and Belle Vue Rangers, St Helens, Warrington and Liverpool City at club level. He won caps for England whilst at Belle Vue Rangers in 1948 against Wales and France and for Great Britain in 1948 in two matches against Australia. Whilst at St Helens Stan played for Lancashire on 8 occasions; for England he won caps against Wales in 1949, France in 1951, Wales in 1953, France (2 matches) and Wales; for Great Britain against Australia in 1949 and between 1952 and 1956 also represented Great Britain while at St Helens between 1952 and 1956 against France.

Stan was 25years old when he transferred from the Manchester based Belle Vue Rangers to St Helens in 1949, for a record fee of £4,000 (£150,000 in purchasing power today) where he reigned, as a star attraction, until moving on to Warrington in 1954. This cracking athlete activated his numerous skills in one of the most prolific periods for class wingers in the game's history in England - the 1950s. In his club career Stan scored 185 tries in 356 games (99 of those tries were with St Helens). In representative games Stan registered 10 tries.

The above mentioned clubs, his County and his Country all saw service from this great wing "character" who was a consistent try - scorer with all the tools of the trade and then some!

MEAKIN Alf: (1938 -)
"The North Shore Flyer"

Illustration by the late
Brian Miller.

Alf was an Olympic sprinter from Blackpool. After the 1964 Tokyo Olympic Games he turned professional and played on trial basis for Leeds. After that he joined his hometown team of Blackpool Borough where he maintained his place in the side for a season. Credited with a 9.4 seconds 100 yards, Meakin was a member of a very good British Sprint Relay Squad which clocked 39.8 seconds for the 4 x 100 metres relay in the 1962 European Championships at Belgrade Yugoslavia, claiming the Bronze medal with Berwyn Jones plus two other Jones boys, Ron and David.

(I competed against Alf Meakin on a regular basis when he was on his way up. Not that I was an Olympic prospect or anywhere near it, but I did make him run all the way, off level and off scratch, in one memorable virtual dead heat sprint when he competed for Blackpool and Fylde A.C. at a Mid - Lancashire League fixture in the late 1950s and, from that personal experience, I can vouch that Alf Meakin certainly could finish – an attribute that is always of value for a winger in Rugby League.)

Make no mistake, Alf was a true sprinter of excellent ability. Compared to some pure sprinters, who tried to convert to Rugby League, Alf was more of a success than was expected, showing a considerable amount of the courage necessary to play this toughest of sports.

MILLWARD Roger: (1947-2016)
"Rodger The Dodger"

With his clubs, Castleford, Hull Kingston Rovers, Cronulla-Sutherland, Roger The Dodger played a total of 461 games and scored 224 tries plus 650 goals.

In representative games of which he totalled for Yorkshire, Great Britain Under 24, England and Great Britain 93 games, he registered 56 tries in a phenomenal career between 1964 and 1979.

Perhaps the most outstanding junior of the T.V. years, this form of the media is in fact where **"Roger The Dodger"** first came to prominence in the 1960s. A Castleford youngster, he was signed up by his hometown club, an era at Castleford which saw the brilliance of the great Alan Hardisty and his scrum half partner Keith Hepworth flourishing.

In the game of Rugby League there have been and still are some "little big men". Millward was very possibly the very best of any era.

At 5ft – 4 ins. tall and under 11 stones, it could be well argued that he wasn't big enough for such a demanding sport. Well, he was!

The other factor of Roger Millward's physical make-up which, in many players of small stature is over - emphasised, was his pace and elusiveness. Lightning sharp off the mark, he was a small player who could eat up the ground and he coupled his electric bursts of pace with an ability to beat defences inside out. Roger had the versatility to play almost any back position and, it could certainly be argued, he was probably the best stand-off/scrum half of any era. He could perform at top level against the very best in either role with great distinction, his devastating speed off the mark being a key factor. Transferred to Hull K.R. early in his career, "The Dodger" scored over 200 tries for the Humberside outfit and, with his successful goal kicking ability, amassed close to 2000 points for the club.

Wingers usually top the Rugby League try scorers list; in 1967-68 Millward topped them all with 38 tries some going for a stand-off half!

In an international career that lasted from 1966 to 1978, Roger Millward made no less than six trips down under and became a great favourite with Aussie fans.

He was a member of the Castleford team that won BBC2 Floodlit Trophies, also playing for Castleford when winning the Yorkshire County Championship.

At the age of 18 he was selected by Great Britain to play against France in 1966.

In August that year he was transferred to Hull Kingston Rovers and immediately the club witnessed the beginning of a transformation – Yorkshire County Cups claimed in consecutive years 1966 and 1967.

In 1968 Roger was selected for the Great Britain Team to play in the 1968 World Cup. Somewhat bizarrely for such a great athlete Roger claimed only two more Yorkshire Cup winner's medals between (1971–76) with Hull K.R. Then In 1976 The Dodger signed for Australian club Cronulla-Sutherland for whom he scored 1 try in 14 games.

On a return to Hull K.R. the BBC2 Floodlit Trophy was taken in 1977 with Roger in the Hull K.R. team. The League Championship was won by Millward led Hull K.R. in 1978-79 for the first time in over half a century; the Challenge Cup Final at Wembley followed 1979-80. Roger led the club to 4 Yorkshire Cup Finals victories. He made 29 Test Match appearances from his 47 appearances for Great Britain and England toured with Great Britain five times and with England once. Even though his contribution was always outstanding a test series win with Roger in the team against Australia proved elusive.

In 2018 a ceremony took place in Hull to rename Garrison Road in honour of Roger-"Roger Millward Way". This diminutive but tough as teak Rugby League great scored a club record 207 tries in 406 appearances for Hull K.R. and kicked 607 goals, was awarded an MBE in 1983 for Services To Rugby League And Sport In Great Britain, and was inducted into the Rugby League Hall of Fame in 2000.

Total respect for this all-time great was shown by Hull Kingston Rovers when they retired his number 6 jersey after his death.

MOIR Ian: (1932 – 1990)
"The Port Kembla Flyer"

Able to sidestep of both feet, Ian, as a youth, was pursued by an athletics coach who tried in vain to persuade him to take up athletics instead of rugby; so fast was Ian Moir and with so much, even Olympic, potential as a track sprinter. As a schoolboy Ian Started to play Rugby League at the age of 15, a student at Wollongong High School, playing at half-back. **On leaving school he played for Port Kembla (NSW), his place of birth, and eventually joined South Sydney Rabbitohs in 1952. Ian Moir, playing for the South Sydney Club, was regarded as the most outstanding find of the season in league circles and made the NSW team.** Actually in his trial match against Western Suburbs he had delighted the crowd with a 70 yards try before being replaced by Australian Test wing Johnny Graves for the final quarter of the match. He had impressed the crowd so much they gave him an unprecedented ovation and they shouted for Graves to leave the field so they could have yet more thrills via this newcomer to the game. It was noted that Moir was very fast off the mark a statement to which I can testify having seen him play. He did however seem to attract a fair amount of injury problems.

Photograph of Ian Moir by kind permission (2012):- "From the collections of the Wollongong City Library and the Illawarra Historical Society" [Wollongong City Council Policy number 9.6]

Ian did play in a rather unique match when he represented an Australasian side against a British Rugby League Thirteen at Bradford's Odsal Stadium in Yorkshire in 1954 and facing him was the great Brian Bevan himself of course an Australian playing for Warrington. The two flyers were the stars of the show with Moir scoring once and "Bev" registering a double in a game won by the Australasian team 24 – 13.

A true International player, Ian represented Australia at the 1954 and 1957 World Cup competitions and in between toured Great Britain with the 1956 "Kangaroos" for whom he topped the try scoring with thirteen. He actually scored 105 tries in just 110 games for his club South Sydney "Rabbitohs". His club career continued with Western Suburbs and his successes in that club's jersey culminated in a two club total 138 appearances and 119 tries. In 23 representative football matches Ian registered 30 tries.

He made eight Test appearances for the Australian national side and represented in four World Cup matches in two World Cups and in 14 Kangaroo tour matches.

Ian was indeed a prodigious try scorer and played in South Sydney's three Premiership victories between 1953 and 1955. In 1953 he scored three tries in the 31–12 Grand Final against St George, capping off a season where he was Souths leading try scorer with a tally of 23. This total stands in 3rd place in the club's all-time list of most tries in a season. He first played for Australia in the inaugural World Cup in France in 1954 and also played Tests against all the rugby league playing nations and toured Great Britain with the 1956 Kangaroos where he played in two Tests and 14 tour matches and as previously stated, topped the tour try scoring list with 13 tries. He featured in Australia's victorious 1957 World Cup campaign played at home. The fastest winger in the Sydney competition was one of six Rabbitohs players to score five tries in a match.

At 5 ft. 6 ins. and a little over 11 stones, Ian was not a big man but he was a true pace merchant and with attacking full back, the legendary Clive Churchill (who many Australians will tell you was the best ever full back) priming him, Moir scored many long distance tries in his career and developed such an uncanny anticipation of just what Churchill might be about to do that, between them, they outwitted many fine defences. He was indeed a professional sprinter who was able to convert track speed into rugby field pace.

Alan Whiticker [sic] of https://www.rugbyleagueproject.org reported that:- *(In 1958 Ian won the NSW Rugby League 110 yards Championship. In full football gear on the Sydney Cricket Ground he clocked 11.1 seconds with Ken Irvine in second place! The race took place prior to the Third Test Match against Great Britain in which Moir played.*

Thirty years later, Ian showed that he had lost none of his old magic when he won the NSW Veterans (50-54yrs) 100m Championship (running 12.7sec.in 1988.)

As a pro sprinter Moir had a top reputation having been credited with well inside "evens" and perhaps an example of his prowess is the fact that as winner of the 1955 prestigious Canberra Gift 130 yards Sprint, nine years later, in 1964, he actually won his semi-final in the same event, only to be disqualified for an infringement.

This 1951 New South Wales Beach Sprint Champion was credited with performances often very much superior to "even time" sprinting.

Circa 31 years of age and running 9.6 or 9.7 pace with ease, apparently not flat out, capable of, in my opinion, around the 12.3 seconds mark or better for 130 yards, how would the "Port Kembla Flyer", who I had first seen 7 years earlier, stand up at say the Stawell Easter Gift celebrations of 1963 or 1964 ?

1963 winner A.J. (John) Bell – ran 12 seconds off 12 yards and 1964 champion Noel Hussey - 12.1 seconds off 8½ yards.

A handicapper using his discretion just might have placed Moir on the 4 yards mark, certainly no worse than 3 yards anyway.

I would submit that in 1963 to match John Bell at Stawell, Ian Moir would have had to produce 6 or 7 yards "inside" and was certainly capable of so doing. In 1964 he would have needed 6 yards "inside" to have challenged for The Gift, an achievement which was surely within the legs of this exceptionally fast rugby league winger.

In 2004 Ian was named by Souths in their South Sydney Dream Team, consisting of 17 players and a coach representing the club from 1908 through to 2004.
An all-time great.

MOUNTFORD Cec: (1919 - 2009)
"The Blackball Bullet"

Just after the second world war, Wigan obtained the services of one Cecil Mountford, a stand-off half from New Zealand. When great stand-offs are spoken of in the Wigan and Warrington areas, for he eventually played for Warrington, the Kiwi's name is put at the very top of the list by many knowledgeable fans of the game. **Cec was also nicknamed "The Blackball Bullet". The Blackball Club in New Zealand having applied that title to him due to his outstanding pace.**

https://stevericketts.com.au/ reminds us that *Blackball, is on the West Coast of New Zealand's South Island. Cec signed with Wigan in 1946, and never got to play for the Kiwis, but captained Other Nationalities teams against England, Wales and France. He also captained 'The Rest' against Great Britain, in the Lord Derby Memorial game, played at Wigan on October 4, 1950. 'The 'Rest' team included Australians, Brian Bevan, Lionel Cooper, 'Wallaby Bob' McMaster and Arthur Clues. Britain won 23-16.*

Cec requested, permission from Wigan to join the 1947- 8 New Zealand tour of Great Britain but the Tour Managers decided not to play him because the squad's injury list was not serious.

Cec Mountford and Wigan Rugby League Club in the 1949-50 season won the Championship Final at Maine Road, Manchester with a 20-2 points defeat of Huddersfield. The great stand-off played at Wembley Stadium in 1948, when Wigan beat Bradford Northern in the Challenge Cup Final and then against Barrow in 1951 with another victory for Wigan, also winning for himself the Lance Todd Trophy on the latter occasion – the first overseas player to do so.

Between 1946 and 1951 The Blackball Bullet had Lancashire County Cup Final victories against Belle Vue Rangers, Warrington twice and Leigh.

At Wembley in the 1951 Challenge Cup Final, I must admit that Cec Mountford was the only stand-off I ever saw get the better of Willie Horne, albeit Wille was behind a beaten pack on the day. But the outstanding feature, to me at least, of Mountford's play was his devastating pace. Only small in stature, he could take off in a long curving run and outpace defences with considerable ease.

There were those fans who compared his pace favourably with that of the great Brian Bevan! "The Blackball Bullet" truly was very fast indeed

In his club career Cec played well over 200 games scoring 70 plus tries. This Rugby League great went on to a major coaching career both with Warrington (first as player/

coach) being offered a 10 year contact and New Zealand. Perhaps the highlight of his coaching in U.K. was in Warrington's 8-4 victory over Halifax in

the 1953–54 Challenge Cup Final replay at Odsal Stadium, Bradford on 5 May 1954 in front of an official record crowd 102,575 but anecdotally more like 120,000. This was a World Record crowd in both of the two codes of the game.

In 1987 the Queen's Birthday Honours list included Cecil Ralph Mountford who was awarded Member of the Order of the British Empire, for Services to Rugby League. In 1990 he was inducted into the New Zealand Sports Hall of Fame then in 2000 he was named as one of the NZRL Legends of League.

MULLINS Brett: (1972 -)

The 6ft 3ins (1.90 m.) 1994 Kangaroo fullback at around the 14 stones (90 kg) mark, may, of course, put the cat amongst the pigeons as far as all of the many Rugby League speed merchants are concerned. Mullins was known for his pace, though he would later state that ....*" I think I used to drink and smoke too much. There's no doubting I had a good time."* The Canberra Raiders/Leeds RLFC/Sydney Roosters/New South Wales/Australia star who scored 139 tries in 240 appearances had the potential, it was thought in Australia, to become their best ever in his position. Apart from his obvious talent as a player, the facet of his athletic prowess most fascinating to me was his apparently raw ability to burn up the grass. It is my opinion that he may well have proven to be the fastest man playing the game in his era anywhere in the world in either code. I would have loved to see him trained up as a sprinter at any of the recognized distances, most of all over 400 metres!

Illustration by the late
Brian Miller.

MURPHY Alex: (1939 –
"Alexander The Great"

Lancashire Schools Rugby League cap sixteen year old Alex Murphy made his debut against Whitehaven at Knowsley Road on 11th April 1956 in a 21 points to 7 win. Even before signing for Saints he was training at the club by invitation of the great coach Jim Sullivan. Sprinting was the order of the day and against senior Saints flyers such as Frank Carlton and Alec Davies. Alex reckoned he held his own against such opposition and, bear in mind, at this time he was still playing rugby for his school St Austins. Jim Sullivan obviously knew there was great advantage to be had by making Alex concentrate on sprinting to improve his already amazing pace. For the next two years Sullivan had him sprinting in training sessions over 30 yard distance marked out by silver paper "jog up to the first then flat out to the second silver paper then ease down". The regime certainly paid off.

(Many thanks are due to Alex Service and Saints Heritage Society who supported my research into Alex Murphy including Stan's photograph.)

Indeed, it was for his school he was playing on the day before his 16th birthday when after the game Saints officials, who were in attendance with those from several other interested clubs, enacted a "vanishing" for the star to be and kept him in a secret location so that he signed for them immediately on becoming sixteen. **The best £80 Saints or any other club ever spent. Yes £80!**

In club football between 1956 and 1975 with Saints, Leigh and Warrington, Alex scored 217 tries in 505 games, 150 goals and 28 drop goals.

In representative games between 1958 and 1971 he registered 54 tries over 67 games playing for Lancashire, England and Great Britain.

Between 1966 and 1994 he coached, Leigh, Warrington, Salford, Wigan,

St Helens and Huddersfield - 1075 games with a 60% win ratio.

Between 1975 and 1988 he coached at representative level Lancashire and England 26 games 62% win ratio.

Books have been written; stories told. You will hopefully excuse me for the amount of detail regarding **"Alexander The Great"** whilst there is certainly even more that chronicles the career of this Rugby genius. I think only Alex is probably capable of telling the full story anyway. One could easily get carried away and lost in the triumphs, and sometimes disasters, of this athlete par excellence.

I'll try to remember that the subject under discussion is pace! Murphy - the greatest scrum half of his or any other era past or present, and, in my opinion unique to the effect that we will never see his like again. At 5ft. 8 inches tall and with a superb physique, Alex Murphy was the ideal rugby league player. I was privileged to see him play many times and I have sympathy for those supporters who have not and have only stories to listen to about this doyen of half backs.

Alexander James Murphy had signed for Saints just after midnight on his sixteenth birthday in 1955 and finished up as a member of Rugby League's Hall of Fame. In between he had toured Australasia twice, the first time in 1958 as a teenager, and played for Great Britain on 27 occasions. He was captain of Saints in their four trophy success season of 1965-66. **In fact, Alex was Saints most successful captain ever. He was also the first player to captain three separate clubs to success in the Challenge Cup Final.**

Scorer of 175 tries for Saints, he went on to play for and coach Leigh to a Challenge Cup Final victory and crowned his career on the field with more Wembley success for Warrington. **As a coach, he has also had tremendous success and there are those who say he should have been given the Great Britain job years ago, but there was something about Alex Murphy that caused the powers that be to refrain from that action. To me, if the man can produce the results that are required, he should be given the opportunity. Sporting politics and diplomacy should play no part in such decisions.**

What was the overriding factor in Murphy's success as a player ? **I would say it was fantastic speed off the mark coupled with enduring accelerating pace and a brilliant rugby brain.** Take away the speed and what have you got ? Half the player he was! I have seen Murphy run from five yards, I have seen him run from 50 yards and when he decided to go from the base of the scrum, generally a try was scored either by Murphy himself or he had so split the defence that one of his supporting threequarters touched down. As previously stated, Murphy was convinced into believing that speed was the key to any success he might achieve by his coach at St Helens, the Wigan legend Jim Sullivan. Sullivan's insistence on the young Murphy improving his powers of acceleration by sprinting between pieces of silver paper from cigarette packets over short distances, repetitively was obviously the key. The benefit was Murphy's and any team he played for.

He could start like a bullet from a gun and this developed talent paid dividends on many occasions. I can see him now in my mind's eye, a little jink to the side and he was off with an electric burst of pace, to such effect that often defences could only watch as he raced to the line. Whilst at Leigh, which, remember, was towards the very end of his career, it is said that he could still beat, over 50 yards, a crack sprinter who was on the books. I can only deduce that the crack sprinter was Rod Tickle and he was truly fast.

Alex also recalled that at Saints over 50 yards he could also match the great Van Vollenhoven.

With Alexander The Great at the helm, from Dec 1968 to Aug 1971 Leigh were undefeated in 44 consecutive home games.

In 1969 - the BBC2 Floodlit Trophy was won by Leigh led by Murphy beating Wigan at Central Park.

In 1970, again led by Alex, Leigh won the Lancashire Cup Final, beating St Helens at Swinton's Station Road stadium.

Alex was awarded the Lance Todd Trophy when he led Leigh to victory in the Challenge Cup Final in 1971 over Leeds.

Signing for Warrington in August 1971 Alex went as player-coach .

In 1974 he captained, at stand-off, the club to a Challenge Cup Final victory over Featherstone Rovers and they had already won three other trophies in that 73-74 season -The Captain Morgan trophy, John Player trophy and the Club Merit trophy.

In 1975 he retired from playing but went on as coach until 1978

In 1998 Alex was awarded the OBE for services to the game of rugby league.

He is also a member of the Rugby League Hall of Fame, St Helens Hall of Fame and the Warrington Wolves Hall of Fame.

Alex Murphy OBE "Alexander The Great", perhaps the finest example of what the development of real pace can achieve for a player's career in this game where athletic prowess can be so very important and is often the difference between victory and defeat.

MURRAY Mike: (1940 -)
"Professor of Pace"

[Photo Supplied by Mike in 1995]

Mike Murray was of course the Rugby League winger representing Barrow RLFC. This excellent athlete signed for the Club in 1963 on the basis that the directors felt his pace would be a great advantage, not only to the organisation, but to himself, in aiding him to make the grade as a League player. "Keeping The Dream Alive" (2008) by Dave Huitson, Keith Nutter and Steve Andrews, the excellent tome, regarding the players who have represented the Club, records that he did indeed make the grade. He represented the first team 168 times scoring 68 tries and played at Wembley in the Rugby League Cup Final. Around the 6 ft. (1.83 m.) mark and 12 stones (76.2 kg.), he produced lightning fast bursts down the left wing for the club who, at the time and possibly in R.L. history, must have had the fastest wing pair in the game, for on the right wing was the lightning fast International Bill Burgess. Unlike other sprinters who have attempted the toughest of all sports, Mike Murray was no "dummy" when it came to skills and guts.

You have to have guts to go onto the park and during the period he played, the game was to say the least a tad over – rough. Sidestep, a great curving swerve and tremendous pace were all parts of this speedster's armoury and he certainly caused every defence he faced to panic whenever he received the ball.

An athlete of rare distinction.

The Other Side of Mike Murray:-

It was 1966 the world famous Powderhall Professional Sprint Championship in Scotland saw the fulfilling of years of preparation for one of the very best sprinters the event had seen before or since, Michael Murray of Barrow RLFC locally born 13th May 1940. Yes, 1966 and Mike Murray's win was a standout in the event's

long history and to many a surprise – to those who were aware of his ability not so much of a surprise but reward for great planning and preparation. This excellent sprinter had spent the better part of twenty years running at professional athletics meetings in and around The English Lake District and Scottish Borders and, in the year that England were to win the Fédération Internationale de Football Association (FIFA) Soccer World Cup, all the work by the sprinter and his associates was to pay off in, perhaps, the crowning glory in the career of a great athlete. **Professor Of Pace - Mike Murray was one of the best exponents I have ever witnessed display the skill of disguising sprinting pace. I reckon he knew, to the inch, just how fast he had to perform in order to satisfy the handicappers and, no doubt, the defences he came up against in Rugby League.**

By the time, late in 1965, the final preparation period came along for what was to prove to be his Powderhall victory, Mike was 25 years of age and, while we're on the subject, the age at which I have always felt a sprinter should come to his best. **He must have been handled admirably by his trainer(s) throughout that part of his career (from 1962 to 1970) in which he was contracted to Barrow Rugby League Football Club. Sprinting ability is an obvious asset in the game, but being a Rugby League player certainly doesn't prepare an athlete to win big sprint events. Even so Mike continued his successful sprinting career during this period.**

The flying rugby league winger completed his preparation in and around the Scottish Borders at The Royal Burgh of Peebles just over 20 miles from Edinburgh spanning the River Tweed and nearby Innerleithen, under the guidance of hosts/associates/trainers Messrs Mac Ballantyne and Eddie Irvine.

On a track reported as being very soft, the Barrow Rugby League Club winger found well supported Rugby Union winger John Smith from Langholm RFC in his heat but came home first clocking 12.07 seconds, from the 4½ yards mark.

Even at this point Mike Murray was very much fancied in the betting, but not considered good enough at that point to win overall, perhaps understandable up to a point considering famed coach Jim Bradley had at least three athletes in the event, all with decent marks.

*[In brief, Jim Bradley was a very successful Scottish coach who had many achievements with sprinters using a boxer's speedball in their training routines, which gained him many followers, both athletes and coaches. Such athletes as **Ricky Dunbar and George McNeill** came under his care, though he was to train many champions both in the UK and abroad.*

In 1963 Dunbar, World Professional 120 Yards Record Holder, was reported as having signed for Wigan RLFC and could have gone on to become the fastest Wigan winger of all time but he chose to go to Australia and contest professional sprinting events.

DUNBAR Ricky

The flying Scot was a full - time athlete and performances which saw him run as much as 9 yards inside "even time".

Dunbar set a World Professional Sprint record at 120 yards and must beg the question, even today, as to just what he might have achieved playing with the Cherry and Whites?

George McNeill *who was, without doubt, one of the fastest men in history actually played a trial game for Barrow RLFC, in September 1972, after being pursued by the late Bill Oxley, the Club Chairman. Even though he was offered a signing on fee, the great sprinter decided that the game really wasn't for him.*

George was very possibly the fastest man in history to play the Greatest Game - amateur or professional. For example, In the heats of the 1971 Powderhall Sprint McNeill clocked 11 seconds dead for 110 metres, off scratch. Remember this event is held at New Year, imagine the temperatures likely to prevail. The result was just shy of 11 yards inside "even time".

Illustration by the late
Brian Miller.

In August 1970 he set a world record for 120 yards at 11.14 seconds, on Meadowbank's tartan track. Had he one regret, I believe it would be that he hadn't started earlier as a sprinter and remained amateur, because he was surely one of the very greatest sprinters of all time. It was just a pity that he decided against signing for Barrow RLFC - he could have been a sensation on the wing.]

Through the rounds and into the final saw Mike Murray running from the 4.5 yards mark as was Ivor McAnany of Blyth, Northumberland ; Billy Edgar of Hawick, Scotland ran from the 7.5 yards mark ; Bob Walker of Dalmeny, Scotland and Murray's sprinting colleague Jim Smith of Barrow both off 8 yards. In fact it was Jim Smith that caused the biggest surprise in the great contest as he made Murray "run for his money", as the saying goes.

The flying rugby league player, who was later to become The British Sprint Champion, clocking a fine 11.42 seconds for his win plus £500 and a Gold medal. (£500 would have the same spending worth today of £9000).

"Honed To Perfection On A Shale Walking Strip" could have been a byline to accompany any description of Mike Murray's sprinting career. In the days before synthetic tracks, indeed before any local track and field facility of any kind was available to Mike, he sharpened his pace and the pace of the athletes who trained with him on what could hardly be termed a pavement or a sidewalk.

In the words of Les Rigg, local bookmaker and athletics sponsor *"Whoever heard of a Powderhall Sprint winner having to train for this golden accolade of professional sprinting on Abbey Road ?"* **(Les was referring to Abbey Road in Barrow in Furness.)**

Yes – people did walk on this particular surface ; a local press item defined such a resource when it highlighted the need for a track in the area by focussing on the facilities used by Mike Murray and his school of professional runners - Abbey Flats - at the outskirts end of Abbey Road, the main road into the town. The shale walking strip, about a quarter of a mile long, was a far distant relative of the athletic tracks of any kind that were springing up all over the country. I was using similar "amenities" for coaching athletes elsewhere in the area and had indeed used the Abbey Flats "Track" on occasions.

One thing has to be said however and that is the very same "facilities" did produce some very fine athletes for example a certain Mike Murray who was surely, in my opinion had he retained amateur status, good enough to have reached an Olympic Sprint Final.

In July 1972 Wakefield Trinity Rugby League Supporters Club staged a "Sports Spectacular" at their Belle Vue ground on Saturday and Sunday 22nd and 23rd of the month. Events ranged through Archery, Amateur and Professional Rugby League Seven a Side, Schools Athletics, Open and Veterans Pro Handicaps, Middle Distance races such as the Horse and Groom sponsored One Mile Open Handicap with one time World record holder Derek Ibbotson down to compete and **The Norman Fox World Professional Sprint Championship - sponsored by Norman Fox Racing Ltd. of Wakefield.**

The athletes who contested the championship were:-

Tommie Smith of San Jose, California, USA. Olympic Champion 200 metres Mexico 1968. Once held 11 World Sprint Records. [At 6ft. 4 inches tall and of well-muscled physique, the San Jose, California athlete of Black Power Salute infamy when he won the 200 metres in the Mexico Olympic Games in 1968 certainly looked as if he could succeed in Rugby League. No one could have any doubts about his speed - 19.8 seconds for 200 metres! The story goes that Wakefield Trinity had brought Smith to the U.K. in 1972 to race against George McNeill, Mike Murray and other top class professional sprinters for the World Championship. However, it is also reported that Trinity had been made aware that Smith had tried his hand at Grid-Iron in the States and felt it was worth paying his expenses to see if they could persuade him to play League. Smith was actually defeated by McNeill over the four race World Championship. As far as the intended attempt to link up Smith with Rugby League was concerned, nothing further occurred.]

Ivor McAnany of Blyth, Northumberland, England
British Champion 120 yards 1969.

George McNeill of Tranent, Scotland
World Professional Record Holder 120 yards.
Winner of 1970 Centenary Powderhall Sprint.

Mike Murray of Barrow in Furness, Lancashire, England
British Champion 120 yards 1966. Winner of 1966 Powderhall Sprint.

Bob Swann of Glenrothes, Scotland
Powderhall Winner 1968. British Champion 110 metres 1971.

The Championship was actually covered by ITV. I was present on the first day. Mike Murray at the age of 32 and arguably well past his best, on a ground in the most atrocious conditions I believe I have ever seen a major sprint event in my life - the long grass and mud of a rugby pitch with right angle turns in the 220 yards, ran second to Olympic 200 metres Champion Tommie Smith and outclassed all of the remaining opposition which included two British 120 yards Champions, a Powderhall winner and World Professional Record Holder, a further Powderhall winner and the winner of Australia's famed Stawell Gift Sprint.

With opposition like that, defeated, no one could argue that the Rugby League winger Mike Murray wasn't very, very fast indeed.

In discussing best performances a conversation I had with Mike in 2010 revealed that he reckoned his best sprints were always about 5 yards inside "even time".

At Jedburgh, running off 1 yard on grass, he was clocked at 9.4 seconds in a 100 yards handicap, equivalent to 10.38 for 100 metres.

In a race against the well thought of Brian Sullivan, Mike gave the former something in the region of 8 yards and beat him over 120 yards with a run 5.5 yards inside "even time".

In "scratch" races over 220 yards / 200 metres Mike was very proud of his performance catalogue which included a win at Meadowbank in a "World Championship" over 220 yards in which he clocked 20.9 seconds in early January in a temperature of minus 8 degrees Centigrade, equivalent to 20.77 sec for 200 metres.

I personally clocked Mike at the Lake District Ambleside Sports on one occasion, as did his colleague George Troth on another occasion, both of us clocked this great athlete at 9.3 seconds running off 1 yard in 100 yards races on an undulating grass track and on the occasion I clocked him he was easing up at the finish!

Mike Murray - A Rugby League flying machine who took on the World's best.

OFFIAH Martin: (1965 -)
"Chariots" Offiah What An Athlete!

With Widnes :-

Rugby Football League Championship First Division
Champions in 1987–88, 1988–89.
Rugby League Premiership Champions in 1987–88, 1988–89, 1989–90.
Lancashire Cup Winners 1990–91.
World Club Challenge Champions 1989.
Rugby League's Man of Steel in 1988. (The only other genuine winger to receive the award was Pat Richards in 2010 as far as I am aware.)
Selected in the 1988 Great Britain Lions tour of Australasia, he played in all three Tests of the Ashes series which was lost.

With Wigan:-

Joined Wigan in 1992 for a World Record fee of £440,000 (Purchasing power today in excess of £1,000,000).
Rugby Football League Championship First Division
Champions in 1992–93, 1993–94, 1994–95.
Rugby League Premiership Champions in 1993–94, 1994–95.
Challenge Cup Winners in 1992–93, 1993–94, 1994–95.
Lancashire Cup Winner in 1992–93.
League Cup Wins in 1992–93, 1994–95.
World Club Challenge Champions in 1994.
Inducted into Wigan Warriors Hall of Fame.

With England:-

Rugby League World Cup Runners Up in 1995.

Awarded the MBE in the 1997 New Year Honours list, Martin was inducted into the Rugby League Hall of Fame in 2013. Voted for by journalists, coaches, players, MPs, national newspaper editors and fans of

the game, a statue is erected outside Wembley Stadium. Eric Ashton, Billy Boston, Alex Murphy, Gus Risman and Martin Offiah are the Rugby League legends that the sculpture features.

Apart from Widnes and Wigan Martin Offiah played in the U.K. for Salford, London Broncos; Eastern Suburbs and St. George Dragons in Australia;

Noted as having registered over 500 tries in his career, his more significant achievements were the 367 scored for Widnes and Wigan (181 for the former).

Thirty three appearances for Great Britain, five for England.

Five tries in the second half against France in 1990/91 season - better than his 10 against Leeds in 1992 in my estimation, just two of the achievements that made the wing ace arguably the best in modern times, certainly in Britain. For a long time after the former R.U. man signed for Widnes, his original club, I was not a "Chariots" fan. Now, even the most unconvinced observer can do no more than at least testify he had the ability to score from anywhere on the field and when, seemingly, there was no chance at all. Coupled with these attributes were other facets of his all - round playing ability and reading of the game that only came with experience. He was no mug where defence was concerned either. Whether he would have been as successful in "the old days" is debatable but one argument is that he may well have been even more so!

A sprint enigma.

During the 1988 Great Britain Lions tour of Australasia, Martin took part in a 100 metres race at Wentworth Park in Sydney against Australian fliers Dale Shearer and John Ferguson. Confirming his standing as the fastest player in rugby league, Offiah easily won the race from Shearer and Ferguson. On the 1992 Great Britain Lions tour of Australasia he took part in a Parramatta Eels pre-match race over 100 metres with Eels flier Lee Oudenryn who won by half a yard. Narrative records that the 6ft 1in (1.85 m.) 14 st. 5 lbs. (91 kg.) flier clocked 10.8 seconds, presumably on a running track, for 100 metres whilst playing for Widnes. *[The Wigan Warriors Miscellany by Ewan Phillips (2010)]*

This kind of pace saw him nicknamed "Chariots" Offiah relating to the film "Chariots of Fire".

"Even timer" – maybe – maybe not!

The flier was reported as having clocked 10.1 seconds for 100 yards, on grass and in rugby boots. London born in 1965, Martin, on Wembley turf carrying the ball, timed over 50 metres in a try scoring effort, which I witnessed, displayed pace that would equate to that of a hand timed 100 metres in 11.04 seconds, which would match up roughly with the times aforementioned. For all his athletic ability and his rugby prowess, I never thought Martin looked like a top class sprinter. Official times seem to be a rarity, if at all available. It is thought by some knowledgeable sources that, had he chosen athletics as a sporting career, he would have been quite successful. Expert sources in Australia offered views that he had never truly unveiled his absolute speed even in training sessions but also that he didn't match up to the conventions of a normal sprinter, an opinion which I endorse in that he always looked awkward to me when in full flight. He himself suggested that there may have been faster wingers. **However, his pace made him so difficult to handle, for any defence, once he was under way and was largely responsible for the tries he scored.**

There was at least one blot on the "Chariots" landscape, appropriately positioned there by one "ET" - Andrew Ettingshausen, who wore the green and gold 29 times for the Kangaroos.

'ET'

Ettingshausen played wing and fullback for Australia and certainly displayed devastating pace, against accepted fliers, on many occasions especially in cover defence situations. As far as ET and Chariots were concerned, in the 1994 Second Test Match at Old Trafford, Manchester, the great centre - three quarter and Kangaroo Captain, Mal Meninga had executed a famous interception and, over virtually the length of the field, was pursued by Great Britain's flying Martin Offiah. Meanwhile, Ettingshausen, who had started some yard or two behind Offiah who was giving everything he had to try and chase down the Australian Captain, never conceded even one inch to the Wigan flyer and actually changed the direction of his run to take a scoring pass from the Australian Captain.

ET had two spells with Leeds where he became a great favourite and was inducted into the Australian NRL Hall of Fame in 2008.

Illustration by the late Brian Miller.

Irrespective of the above incident Martin Offiah's pace made him so difficult to handle, for any defence, once he was under way and was largely responsible for his immense try scoring totals.

Martin Offiah - An absolute Rugby League and sporting legend in the truest sense.

133

PRESTON Mark: (1967 -)
"007"

The aforementioned "007" had nothing to do with being a Royal Navy Commander doubling as a secret intelligence service agent, but in the case of one stylish character Mark Preston, from the realms of commerce related to insurance, it was one of two nicknames (the other being "Bond") apparently given to him by Wigan three-quarter Joe Lydon when the ex-Preston Grasshoppers, Fylde and England Rugby Union "B" team speedster played for the Wigan outfit. Mark had scored almost 100 tries before he turned to Rugby League.

Then at Wigan he registered 57 tries in 77 games between 1987 and 1990;

90 tries in 134 games for Halifax 1991-1996; with Widnes 4 tries in 1996 over 8 appearances. **I am sure there was never any doubt about his pace at Wigan, where he had the crowd on their toes whenever he touched the ball, for he was tremendously fast.** From Wigan he went to Halifax for a £65,000 fee, where he played five years and I'm confident that the historic club's historian, Andrew Hardcastle, likewise, never had any doubts about Preston's sprinting abilities.

No doubt there are supporters of the game who will say that there have been faster men than Mark Preston in the game of Rugby League but in my opinion he could match many of them. Preston was involved in athletics whilst at school and clocked fast times, but more importantly, he always realised the importance of this facet of his abilities to his overall impact as a winger and, therefore, worked at his speed development with expert coaching. **Preston clocked 10.7 seconds for 100 metres on more than one occasion, a time which underpins what every League follower knows, that it was madness to give him any start at all or the ball would be touched down under the posts. In my opinion, this athlete transferred his track speed onto the rugby field without much loss of pace and would rank with the very best of any era of the game regarding pace.** A "Top O'The Ground" Pace Merchant was Mark Preston - my purely personal opinion that he was much better on hard grounds than in the mud and mire which did undoubtedly hinder some wingers less than others in the game of Rugby League.

RING Johnny: (1900 – 1984)

"He seemed the fastest thing on two legs in the world."
(former Wales R.U. cap and 1938 GB tourist, Vivian Jenkins)

Prior to Billy Boston another Welshman held the try scoring record at Wigan. Johnny Ring played for the Central Park outfit throughout the 1920s and was a great favourite with the crowds. Formerly with Aberavon R.U. Club, **Ring was Rugby League's leading try - scorer for four seasons in succession in his time at Wigan.** This Welsh flier gained international honours and was a member of the successful 1924 Lions Tour Squad to Australia.

With Wigan Johnny registered 368 tries in 331 games between 1922-1931 then he played for Rochdale Hornets between 1932-1934 scoring 12 tries in 26 games. At representative level he played 7 times for Wales touching down 5 tries. On the 1924 Lions tour to Australia Johnny scored 21 tries in 14 games and in the Tour trial 1 try for Stripes versus Whites. He also played in a Test match at Wigan in 1926 against New Zealand.

Glamorgan & Monmouthshire was competing in the Rugby League County Championship in the late 1920s and Johnny Ring played 8 times for the club scoring 5 tries.

County Cup Finals, Challenge Cup Finals and Championship Finals played a prominent part in this fine athlete's history.

I have unearthed no actual recorded times for sprinting achieved by Johnny but in addition to Vivian Jenkins quote in full below consider Ewan Phillips description " **The greyhound like Johnny Ring….**" from his The Wigan Warriors Miscellany (The History Press 2010) and in his Union days when Rugby had resumed after World War One Aberavon RFC noted that "A new wing emerged, Johnny Ring. He was quickly noted as both a flier and a fine footballer of pace. He bagged 38 tries in season 1919-20." From the history of Aberavon RFC, Former Wales cap and 1938 British Lions R.U. tourist to South Africa,

Vivian Jenkins, wrote in The Sunday Times in 1976:- *"It was sometime in the winter of 1920-21 that I first caught sight of Aberavon, playing in those days at the Old Mansel Field, now Sandfields. I was one of a group of small boys who crawled through a gap in a corrugated fence to get a free view of the men soon to become my heroes. Legendary wing Johnny Ring was the talk of the town at the time and he seemed the fastest thing on two legs in the world. Fast he must have been because he was the highest try scorer in the club history and I was thrilled when he was capped against England at Twickenham in 1921. Wales lost 18-3, but Johnny got Wales's only score - a try. It broke my heart when he went over to Rugby League soon afterwards and I believe I shed tears of despair. But for me Johnny is still the Bravon Boy that I used to sing about in the old war song."*

ROBINSON Jason (1974 –
"Billy Whiz"

An incredibly elusive 5ft. 8ins. (1.73m.) 12 st. 11 lbs.(81kg) of pace.

Another great athlete of the smaller variety who could really motor. He shocked many fancied speed merchants certainly on the field of play.

Wigan's pocket dynamo Jason (Billy Whiz) Robinson I honestly believed early in his career was the classic case of playing people out of position. As did Wigan, thoughts at one time were Jason would be a budding half-back, just as I thought myself.

[Billy Whizz is a fictional character from the comic "The Beano" - a boy who can run extremely fast.]

History shows that, as everyone interested in Rugby League or Rugby Union knows, he made the grade as an international wingman and scored some excellent tries from often impossible positions when receiving the ball. Jason basically had all the attributes - great speed off the mark, possibly the fastest acceleration ever seen in the game, impressive pace in full flight and was amazingly elusive. Jason recorded a time of 10.67 seconds for 100 metres.

In League 171 tries in 281 games, victories in the Regal Trophy (3); Rugby League Challenge Cup Finals (3); League Championship on 8 occasions and the Super League Championship. In Wigan's victory he was awarded the Harry Sunderland Trophy as man-of-the-match. That year -1998- he was also named on the wing in the season's Super League Dream Team, and again in the following two seasons. Billy Whiz was in the Wigan team that beat Brisbane Broncos at Lang Park in 1994 to become World Club Champions.

He won 12 caps for Great Britain and seven for England. At age19 he played for Great Britain against New Zealand.

In 2000 Jason switched codes and joined Rugby Union's Sale Sharks, going on to play 159 games for them, scoring 248 points. He also played for Bath and Fylde and won 51 international caps for England. He actually played more games from full back than from the wing for England and was equally if not more devastating from that position. He was the first black man to captain the England team. Scored a decisive try against The Wallabies in the 2003 World Cup winning England team. He scored 30 tries in international matches and played in all of England's World Cup games that year.

Jason also appeared for The British & Irish Lions in 5 Test matches during the 2001 and 2005 tours.

Johnny Wilkinson is recorded as commenting that:- *"**His ability to beat players both ways, and make 90-degree direction changes without losing speed, obliterated what I believed were the limits for footwork and speed.**"*

In New Year Honours Lists Jason was awarded the MBE for his part in the team that won the 2003 World Cup and in 2008 the OBE for services to Rugby.

ROSENFIELD: Albert "Rozzy": (1885-1970)

Australian Rugby League (Kangaroos) who toured England in 1908-09
(Photo from State Library of Queensland www.slq.qld.gov.au/)

Back row - Alf Dobbs, Alex Burdon, Peter Moir, Pat Walsh, Dan Frawley, Sid Deane, Jim Abercrombie, **Albert Rosenfeld**.

Second row - John Rosewell, Billy Cann, Tom McCabe, Jack Fihelly, W. S. Noble (Secretary), Bill Hardcastle, Sandy Pearce, James W. Davis, Lou S. Jones, Bob Graves.

Third row - Bill Heidke, Charlie Hedley, Jim Devereaux, H. H. Messenger (Vice-Captain), James Giltinan (founded the NSWRL), Denis Lutge (Captain), Albert R. Conlon, Thomas A. Anderson, Larry O'Malley.

Front row - William Bailey, Tedda Courtney, Michael M. Bolewski, Arthur Butler, Arthur Halloway, Arthur Hennessy, Andrew D. Morton, Frank Cheadle.

Inset - Arthur Anlezark.

The Kangaroos sailed on RMS Macedonia and worked as stokers to keep their fitness levels up. The jerseys were coloured sky blue and maroon, combining the state colours of NSW and Queensland respectively. The J. J. Giltinan Shield is currently presented to the National Rugby League's "Minor Premiers".

The following is information extracted and paraphrased from

The Players Archive by David Gronow:-

www.huddersfieldrlheritage.co.uk/Archive/Written/Players/Albert_Rosenfeld.html

Albert "Rozzy" Rosenfeld played rugby union as a teenager in the eastern suburbs of Sydney where he represented Eastern Sydney Borough until 1907 when he became aware of the "rugby revolution" taking place in New South Wales and it was then that he "turned to the new type of rugby football." In August 1907 including "Rozzy" the New Zealand tourists, known as Baskerville's "All Golds", were notable in the fact that none of them had ever played the "new game".

Author's Note:

Albert Henry Baskerville

[It was he who practically originated the professional Rugby movement in Australasia

— The Sydney Mail, 27 May 1908

Prior to becoming the administrator of the 1907-08 tour, Baskerville played rugby union He was said to be on the verge of provincial selection. Baskerville took part in many athletic events from 1903 to 1907 as a runner competing for prize money.

He became nationally famous through his book "Modern Rugby Football: New Zealand Methods; Points for the Beginner, the Player, the Spectator", published in 1907, after which he came up with the idea of a professional rugby tour of Great Britain. He contacted the Northern Union and asked if it would host a touring party of New Zealand rugby players to which request the Northern Union agreed.

He received a life ban from the New Zealand Rugby Union but still assembled a touring party which included 8 All Blacks from the 1905 tour of Great Britain. The Sydney Press christened the tourists as the "All Golds" intending to belittle the New Zealand Rugby Union.

The tour was a great success both financially (each player earned roughly £300 circa £33,000 purchasing power today) and on the field, where the touring side won consecutive Test series against Great Britain and Australia.

Sadly Baskerville contracted pneumonia on the ship taking the touring party from Sydney to Brisbane and, after several days in hospital, died aged 25 in Brisbane on 20 May 1908.]

En-route to England, the tourists played three matches in Sydney against New South Wales and because none of the New Zealanders had ever played under any laws except Rugby Union the games were played under Union laws.

At the Royal Agricultural Ground on 17 August, with 22,000 spectators present, NSW were victors by 11 points to 8. The tourists thus banned themselves from Rugby Union. In that game "Rozzy" played stand-off.

The 'All Golds', on their return from Britain, were in Sydney to play a three-match series - they were the first Test matches to be staged in the Southern Hemisphere, "Rozzy" played all three games and scored a try in the first Test in a 11-10 defeat by New Zealand.

Regarding Rosenfeld's signing for Huddersfield - after the Tourists had played at Huddersfield on 20th February 1909 he became a registered Fartowner along with forward "Paddy" Walsh. It would appear that the "stand-off" was seriously being considered as a winger at Huddersfield.

After returning to Australia for a short period "Rozzy" was back at Fartown by August 1909 and made his debut on the right wing against Broughton Rangers on 11th September 1909 scoring a try.

David Gronow records:-

He scored 22 tries from 35 appearances in 1909/10 and 35 the following season (1910/11) then established a new try record in 1911/12 when he ripped up the record books with seventy-eight tries, eclipsing the record for tries in season which stood at 49 jointly held by Wigan's England winger Joe Miller and Halifax's Welsh international Billy Williams who both performed the feat in 1908/09.

Rozzy played twice for a Colonial XIII against the returning 1910 Tourists, his only representative games during his time in England - at Headingley on 19 September in a 31pts-15 win, and at Wigan on 27 December, Rosenfeld scoring his first hat-trick of tries on English soil in a 22pts-40 loss. On Boxing Day 1911, he performed his best match feat in registering eight tries against Wakefield Trinity.

Rozzy - as he was affectionately known by Huddersfield supporters - began to score tries at an alarming rate - 269 in 158 in the next four seasons. In 1912/13 he managed a mere fifty-six, but the following season he was to cut loose in a manner that has never been equalled before or since.

In 1913/14, his total of 80 tries from 42 games set up a rugby league record that is likely to stand forever - the closest tally was by Brian Bevan who scored seventy-two in 1952/53. **Rozzy was the perfect running machine at the end of an inspired back line,** *and scored 7 tries in a 119-2 demolition of Swinton Park in a Challenge Cup-tie on 28 February 1914 - the* **'Team of All Talents'** *winning all four trophies available to them in that record-breaking season of 1914/15, Rozzy ending it with a tally of 55 tries. In his career at Fartown, he scored 5 tries on twelve occasions, 4 tries eight times and 3 tries twenty-seven times and topped the Rugby League try-scoring charts in four successive seasons from 1911/12 to 1914/15.*

The First World War interfered with his career – he served in Mesopotamia (Iraq) - therefore its anyone's guess just what else he may have achieved in Rugby League had that not been the case. In a cup tie against Leeds "Rozzy" played his last game for Huddersfield on April 2nd 1921. Described in the Huddersfield Examiner as "the wary, nippery, slippery little Australian" Rozzy had notched up 366 tries in 287 games for the club.

In September 1921 he was transferred to Wakefield Trinity and played for Trinity 66 games registering 16 tries in two seasons, then he signed for Bradford Northern clocking up 1 try in 23 games. The Colonial X111, for which he played twice, saw him score 3 tries. [Rosenfeld had also played 15 games for the Australians in England and Wales in 1908/09, scoring 5 tries.]

In summary:- It is said that the greatest Rugby League team of all time was the Huddersfield squad in the years just before the First World War and in this **"Team Of All Talents"** was Australian flying wingman, Albert Rosenfeld.

He was described as **"devastatingly clinical for a winger of his size - 5ft. 6inches (1.68m.) and 12 stones (76.2 kg.)"**.

During "Rozzy's career with the Fartowners the club had one of the all-time great centre partnerships in the form of Harold Wagstaff and Tom Gleeson and during "Rozzy's" all - time season total effort of 80 tries, the astonishing fact is that his centre, Gleeson, also totalled 47 tries!

Albert Rosenfeld was inducted as one of the original nine entrants into the Rugby Football League Hall of Fame on 24 October 1988, similarly one of 21 initial players introduced into the Huddersfield RL Club Players Association Hall of Fame on 22 April 1999.

His name had been etched for all time in the annals of Rugby League when he played for Eastern Suburbs (Easts) on Easter Monday 20th April 1908 in the original matches played in Australia. Easts beat Newtown by 32 -16 at Wentworth Park with "Rozzy" playing stand-off.

Albert "Rozzy" Rosenfeld passed away on 4 September 1970 aged 85 and at the time E.E.Christensen in the Sydney Daily Telegraph remarked:-"Rosenfeld achieved football immortality in Australia and England and was a remarkable man both in youth and old age. His record has never been approached and, nowadays, English club wingers feel proud of themselves if they can manage thirty tries in a season."

The Huddersfield Daily Examiner simply quoted:
"He was one of the most famous of all Rugby League players."

RYAN Bruce: (1921 - 2002)

Bruce Ryan scoring his debut try against Castleford 23rd August 1947
(Photo supplied by Colin Booth who also assisted in my research.)

One of the very first names that comes to mind from when I started to watch Rugby League is Australian Bruce Ryan playing for Hull F.C.. I must have been 8 years of age.

Bruce, of the Newtown Club, New South Wales was also a very fine runner.

In 1939, at the GPS athletic meeting at Newtown, Bruce Ryan was the shining light. [The Athletic Association of the Great Public Schools of New South Wales (AAGPS) which is a sporting association of boys schools in New South Wales, Australia that contest sporting events among themselves. The AAGPS was formed on 30 March 1892.]

{An Australian press report stated that Bruce made even time in the 220 yards, and ended in a great sprint in the relay race to win for his college, then turned round and stripped for the 440 yards, which he won.
Bruce had also equalled Jimmy Carlton's famous 100 metre record.
In 1925-27 Carlton had taken the senior treble at the Great Public Schools' championships, establishing records in all three events. In 1927 he became the first schoolboy in New South Wales to run 100 yards in 10 seconds, and on the same day ran 220 yards in 21.8 seconds: both records lasted twenty-nine years. That year Carlton was the youngest athlete to that time

to win the two sprints at the New South Wales and Australian championships. He repeated the double in 1928 and 1929.

At the 1928 Amsterdam Olympic Games, Carlton failed to reach top form because of illness and was defeated in the 100 and 200 metres semi-finals. In 1931 at Newcastle, New South Wales, he equalled Eddie Tolan's world record of 9.4 seconds for 100 yards, but the run was not recognized as there were only two timekeepers. However, in December 1930 at the Sydney Cricket Ground he set an Australian record, which lasted twenty-three years, of 9.6 seconds. In January 1932 at the Australian Championships he ran 220 yards in 20.6 seconds on a curved grass track, but the time was not recognized because of wind assistance. He was also a successful Rugby Union wing three-quarter, playing for St Joseph's College, and for New South Wales in 1930}.

I record the foregoing on Jimmy Carlton as a comparative measure of just how fast Bruce Ryan was.

Certainly in 1944 he was regarded as Rugby League's fastest winger in Australia.

In 1941 at the age of 18 Ryan had joined the Army and served in Papua New Guinea. Whilst on leave from the Army he continued to play for his Newtown club. When he returned to his unit in P.N.G. he was a malaria victim and his illness robbed him of a place in the Australian Test team against Gus Risman's Tourists. So illness kept him out of Test matches.

Ryan had only to be fit and well to walk into any side with his physique at height 5 foot 11 inches(1.80 m.) weight l3st. 5 lbs. (84.8 kg.) The Sydney Daily Telegraph said, **"Tackling Ryan is like trying to stop a tank."**

Bruce Ryan signed for Hull FC for the 1947- 48 season at a fee of four figures and arrived at Paragon Station to be met by Hull FC officials, players and a reported 4,000 supporters. He quickly settled into the team and was a great success playing on the wing; his playing record for "The Airlie Birds" was 84 matches and 60 tries in the 3 seasons he played for them. At Ryan's own request he was put on the transfer list for the 1950-51 season, for Leeds to sign him.

[Raymond Fletcher, admired authority on the game, says: Ryan played for Hull from 1947 to 1950. Scored 60 tries in 84 matches. Transferred to Leeds in 1950 for a then record £4,750 and scored 42 tries in 57 matches over two seasons.]

[Authors Note: "The Airlie Birds" - related to Airlie Street in West Hull.]

Then, it was a great shock to Leeds when they discovered that Bruce was on a ship together with his wife and children to go back to Australia. Incidentally throughout his stay in Yorkshire he had built up a reputation of being a singer with a dance group. He later joined the coaching staff of North Sydney in 1956. Ryan died on 25 June 2002, 12 days before his 81st birthday.

SOUTHWARD Isaac (Ike) (1934 – 2006)
"Cumberland Express"

On 29th. July, 1952 Ike Southward signed for Workington Town. On March 11th. 1959, a world record transfer fee was paid by Oldham to Town, of £10,650 for Ike's services. However, via a gentleman's agreement that if Ike wanted the move and Town could afford him then he would make the move back to Derwent Park. The deal stood at £11,002.10s which was 50 shillings more than St Helens paid Wigan for Mick Sullivan. So the world record was broken again for Ike to make his second Town debut where he continued to play until 21st October 1968. At Oldham Ike had registered 54 tries in 52 games.

About to make a tackle at Wembley Stadium in 1958 v Wigan. A game in which Ike's deceptive, but remarkable pace, was obvious. Ike scored a try and 3 goals for all Workington Town's points in their 13-9 defeat.(From a photo supplied to me by Ike in 1995)

In 1955 Ike ran in 7 tries and 6 goals for Town against Blackpool Borough and in a match with a Warrington team containing the great Brian Bevan he scored 5 tries.

During his National Service Ike also represented the British Army at Rugby Union.

By the end of the 1950s Ike was regarded in the top echelon of the Rugby League's wingers Eventually he also turned out for Town's neighbours Whitehaven, played 6 times and left the game on 1st February 1969.

This Cumbrian wingman, from a League background at junior club Glasson Rangers before turning pro, scored 274 tries in Town's colours which represent the club's record total. Southward was a more than useful tackler and a very reliable goal - kicker.

A member of Ashes - winning touring teams in 1958 and 1962, Ike was an impressive and long - striding flier in an era of great and very fast wing three quarters. Ike had clocked 9.9 seconds for 100 yards in the British Army Championships in the early 1950s. Reared in Ellenborough, Cumberland, England, Ike Southward was naturally talented, tremendously fast ; like a greyhound, a winger who could, pace

for pace, match them all, with a unique defence deceiving change of pace and an ability to finish a move better than most. Indeed if there is an animal that Ike's style of running could have been likened to, it would be a greyhound or a cheetah – low to the ground and long striding.

This Cumberland wingman actually started for Workington Town as an eighteen year old stand-off half, with then coach the great Gus Risman reputedly being responsible for turning Ike into the flying winger he promptly became. Ike played seventeen years at professional level.

Ike represented Cumberland on 14 occasions scoring 6 tries and 2 goals.

Having played for England U21's v France at Avignon in 1954 this Ashes winning tourist in 1958 (when he scored in all three Test matches) and 1962, represented Great Britain on eleven occasions, facing France, Australia and New Zealand ; he also played exhibition Rugby League in South Africa. Cumberland County saw service from this impressive athlete on thirteen occasions.

When playing for Workington Town, Ike and Australian centre Tony Paskins, recruited from Sydney's Randwick Rugby Union Club,were a formidable pair for any defence to face - one of the most feared duos in the game.

In "retirement" from the game Ike Southward took up coaching in the amateur scene then with Workington, Whitehaven and Cumbria.

Town now take on Whitehaven annually at the beginning of the season for the Ike Southward Memorial Trophy. Ike was inducted into the Workington Town Hall of Fame just prior to his passing and acknowledged as one of the best wingers in the world. Many tributes were paid to this great athlete on his passing and perhaps that of Bill Wookey, former team mate who played centre to Ike at club level and went on the 1958 tour with him, is an excellent example of many:-

"I played my best rugby league with Workington Town and the first thing you would say about Ike Southward, outside of how great a winger he was, was that he just loved a joke. There were so many great tries that it's hard to single out one in particular. I remember the seven he scored against Blackpool because I was our other try scorer that day. I would put him in the top eight of all the great wingers. On the 58 tour he was always a popular character and everybody loved the way he spoke. He was an honest man and a good man."

STOPFORD John: (1936 – 1998)

John Stopford, Wigan born and bred, I saw many times as he graced that wonderful Swinton side of the late 1950s and early 1960s which was, in my opinion at least, a footballing outfit, comparable with the Huddersfield and Wigan teams of the era. Swinton had the arts of passing and backing up off to perfection and often ran opposing teams ragged. In this classy group of players was a left winger who, incidentally, had been turned down by Wigan after trials, John Stopford. He played several positions with Swinton until he eventually settled on the wing.

Not a tall man but of very muscular physique, possibly due to his days as an Army P.T. Instructor, Stopford was a very tricky and dangerous customer. In 1963-64 season he recorded a Swinton club record with 42 tries. John touched down 195 times in 298 appearances for Swinton.

John Stopford scores for Swinton
[Photo supplied by John in 1995]

In time he gained international honours in addition to touring in the Ashes losing Great Britain team of 1966. This accomplished flier represented Lancashire on 5 occasions scoring 1 try. John won caps for Great Britain in 1961 and in 1963 plus against Australia in 1963. The following year saw him gain further caps against France then in 1965 against France again plus New Zealand. More representative honours came his way again in 1966 against France and in the 1966 Great Britain Lions tour in Australia. Appearing 12 times in G.B. jersey John Stopford scored 7 tries.

John Stopford had the ideal natural gifts for sprinting, he could move his arms and legs very quickly indeed and was very successful on the track in his Army days.

SULLIVAN Clive MBE: (1943 – 1985)
Twice A Legend – Talent and Pace

By kind permission of Hull F.C.
Official Facebook

Welshman Clive Sullivan was another wing wizard. More in the mould of Halifax's Johnny Freeman than of Bouncing Billy Boston and he was a great favourite with the Humberside supporters, having actually had great success playing for both Hull F.C. and Hull K.R. His career was to be troubled by injuries, both on and off the field, that would have finished many a lesser man but this didn't stop Sullivan. **He became a feared international flier, for flier he was and, though I have no actual sprint times for Sullivan, he was recognised everywhere he played as a man not to give half a yard of space to or he would be under the posts.**

Again, an example of a winger who could produce devastating pace carrying the ball. Coupled with a destructive sidestep, in the Brian Bevan style, his outstanding pace was something to be dealt with quickly by opposing defences or rue the moment he was given any opportunity at all. Probably the best remembered try he ever scored at international level was in the World Cup Final in France in 1972 at Lyon's Stade De Gerland Stadium on November 11th when, as captain of Great Britain against Australia, he produced a near length of field effort to touchdown, displaying all of his defence deceiving talent and pace.

"Twice A Legend" : It is a mark of the man that he played for both clubs in the Humberside City of Hull (Hull F.C. and Hull Kingston Rovers), was an outstanding success with both of these, arguably the most fierce rivals in any sport, certainly in the Rugby League game in England, and yet remained just as popular with each set of supporters even after he had left "their" club - unquestionably a legend at both.

An out and out sprinter with blistering pace his trademark, this accomplished athlete, Welsh born in 1943, signed for Hull FC and played from 1961, for 13 seasons at The

Boulevard. Against Doncaster in 1968 Clive registered 7 tries in one game. In 1974 he transferred across the City of Hull to Hull Kingston Rovers where he registered 118 tries in 213 games for the red and whites. He also played a short time for Oldham in Lancashire 18 games – 3 tries and Doncaster in Yorkshire 9 games, before returning to the black and white colours of Hull FC for which club, in his career, he scored a total of 250 tries in 352 games, including seven in one game against Doncaster.

The Welsh Rugby League Hall of Fame records that :-

He won the first of 17 caps for Great Britain in 1967, playing three World Cup matches in 1968 with a hat trick in the game against New Zealand. He toured Australia a year later, but injury restricted him to just one Test. Returning to Great Britain in 1971 he appeared in all three Tests against New Zealand and in 1972 was awarded the captaincy for the two Tests with France. As captain of the team which won the World Cup in France in 1972, Clive scored a try in each of Great Britain's four games. His Great Britain career finished in 1973 with three Tests against Australia. In his 17 appearances he had scored 13 tries and captained the side on nine occasions.

With Wales he won 15 caps in the period 1968-1979.

In all games, club and international, he scored 406 tries in 639 appearances, a record bettered by only two other Welshmen and only half- a-dozen players of any nationality. He will always rank as one of the greatest finishers in the game of Rugby League

Clive also became the original black sportsman to captain any national sporting team when he captained Great Britain on the first of nine occasions.

This feared international flyer was recognised everywhere he played as a man not to be given half a yard of space or he would be under the posts.

Clive Sullivan's ability as a track sprinter is perhaps best illustrated by considering the Jedburgh Border Games of 1966 where in the £150 Jedforest 120 Yards Open Handicap Sprint and the Invitation 120 Yards Sprint he was up against athletes of the calibre of :-

British Champion and fellow Rugby League player Mike Murray of Barrow in Furness, Lancashire ;

Ivor McAnany of Blyth, Northumberland, a former winner of The Jedforest and a future (1969) British Champion at 120 yards; local to Jedburgh ;

John Steede who was to become an athletics legend in Scotland and who took out the Invitation 120 Yards Sprint that year, the Jedforest Handicap in 1963 and would again in 1972 ;

British Olympic sprinter Alf Meakin of Blackpool, plus other fine speed merchants.

In the year when England won the Soccer World Cup, Rob Bannon of Jedburgh, won that **£150 Jedforest Open Handicap Sprint** prize. The finish put in by Bannon to win the 120 yards handicap from a start of 10 yards set the big crowd roaring when he broke away from the challenge of the opposition which included top marker Peter Pye from Sunderland who finished 2nd; Ivor McAnany of Blyth in 3rd place and ; Clive, off a mark of 5 yards, in 4th place. It appears from photographic evidence I have seen that McAnany managed to pass Clive virtually on the tape.

Ivor McAnany, the Blyth flyer, off 1 yard, was clocked at 4 yards "inside" evens with Clive, who challenged for the lead 20 yards from the finish, so close he must have been on "evens" or just "inside" considering the handicaps.

In 1974 Clive was awarded the M.B.E.

The final section of the A63 road into Hull was renamed "Clive Sullivan Way" in honour of the greatly respected athlete who passed away in 1985 at an age of 42 years.

SULLIVAN Mike: (1934 – 2016)

Huddersfield, Wigan, St Helens, York, Dewsbury, 218 tries in 390 games.

Yorkshire, England, Great Britain, Great Britain & France, Rugby League X111, 125 tries in 110 games.

To be described as quick, direct and decisive and scoring well over 300 tries, in an era when there was a surfeit of class wingmen, is, at least, a fair testimony to the skills and pace of Mick "Sully" Sullivan. A plumber by trade, he also served his apprenticeship in the toughest of all sports and became a household name in the game of rugby league, revered by some of the game's followers and hated by others. His determination to more than play his weight was known worldwide and was undoubtedly the reason, on occasions, that he found the disfavour of referees and opposing

"Sully"
The Great Winger in Action
(Supplied to me by Mike in 1996)

supporters. The Yorkshireman as a centre, was a position which Sully could also fill with distinction.

Pound for pound, the toughest wingman of his era and, for my money, the toughest I have ever seen. At a bodyweight under 12 stones and 5 ft 8 inches tall he played as if he was 6 ft. 3 inches tall and 15 stones and the international left winger was the scourge of Club, County, Australian, Kiwi and French opposition for many years.

His speed, presence of mind and football awareness were factors which kept him in the forefront of world rugby during a career that saw him become without doubt the most successful left winger, certainly at international level, of all time.

A World Cup winner in 1954, he appeared in three Rugby League World Cups (1954, 1957, and 1960), helping Great Britain to the title in both 1954 and 1960. He played in 46 Tests and scored 41 tries. Sully set the record for most Great Britain caps with 46, which was later matched by Garry Schofield. On the 1958 tour he scored 38 tries in 19 matches!

"Sully" went from Huddersfield, his original club, to Wigan for a then world record fee of £9,500, to Saints for £11,000 then spells with York and Dewsbury and in Australia.

He had an amazingly successful career which, coincidentally, had started out by him playing centre to one of the acknowledged all - time greats, Lionel Cooper. Perhaps he learned something from the Aussie about running quickly, directly and decisively!

"A difficult man to stop, possessing pace, strength and a side-step to match the best. And then there was that brutal defence. Mick Sullivan was one of the toughest players the game has ever seen, a man who played with such enthusiasm and commitment that the opposition knew they were in for a hard time as soon as the whistle blew. When he retired from the game opposition players must have breathed a sigh of relief that this true man of steel had hung up his boots. Even in his latter playing career, 'Sully' let you know that he was on the pitch."

Mike "Stevo" Stephenson – Sky T.V.

Mike Sullivan was inducted into The Rugby League Hall of Fame in 2013.

THOMAS Dai: (?- ?)

With a valid reputation as a track sprinter Dai Thomas had the status of being the fastest footballer, in either rugby or soccer, when joining Halifax in 1907. He played on the wing at representative level for Wales, and a Welsh League XIII, and at club level for Dewsbury and Halifax.

At Dewsbury Dai holds the "Tries In A Season" record with 40-tries scored in the 1906–07 season, and the "Tries In A Match" record with 8 tries against Liverpool City on 13 April 1907.

The flyer won 3 caps for Wales and scored 3 tries while at Halifax in 1908 against England and represented a Welsh League XIII in their 14–13 victory over Australia at Penydarren Park, Merthyr Tydfil on Tuesday 19 January 1909.

Photo of the Welsh flyer from circa first decade of 20th century.

TICKLE Rod: (Circa 1945 -)

Rod made his debut for Leigh RLFC on 10th November 1962.

Between 1962 and 1972 he played 284 games and scored 114 tries and also played once for Great Britain at under 24 level.

The Leigh winger was a holder of an English Schools Athletics Association high jump record and, eventually, turned out to be one of the fastest men ever to play the game of Rugby League. It is reported that Tickle perhaps fell between two stools and had he chosen to stick with athletics, instead of trying to mix it with another sport, could have been phenomenal as a track sprinter. As it was, in the 1967 Powderhall Sprint, the eventual winner, Eddie Cain, was receiving a start from Tickle, an odds on favourite, and was only victorious by the narrowest of margins. **Rod could run well inside "even time", in fact his performance in the Powderhall against Cain was worth inside 9.5 seconds for 100yards!**

Illustration by the late
Brian Miller.

The Powderhall New Year Sprint Handicap had developed into The Skol New Year Sprint or The Skol Powderhall New Year Handicap, which was first contested in 1965, when the Skol Company became involved in sponsoring the classic professional sprint event.

It was the third year of the Skol sponsorship that found this talented athlete, under the guidance of experienced and respected trainer Matthew Clamp of Brighouse in Yorkshire, attempting to take home the most prestigious professional sprint prize in the United Kingdom. Running out of Newton-Le-Willows, Lancashire, England, Rod found amid his challengers, from over 20 heats where there was a lot of money lost and won, for the big sprint prize in 1967 included - Eddie

Cain of Carlisle, Cumberland, simply regarded a beginner, but one who could obviously run. In his semi - final whilst Cain was triumphant, Rod ran in as a very easy winner in his semi in such style that it was bound to influence the betting odds for the final, even though by then he had become very much odds on.

Consider that New Year's Day in 1967 was one of the coldest for 16 years. Fast sprinting in such an environment is admirable witness to the preparation of the athletes and the astuteness of their coaches.

The 1967 line up for the final of The Skol New Year Handicap of 120 Yards, held at Powderhall, was :-

Billy Edgar of Hawick, Roxburghshire, Scotland off 7½ yards

Dave Campbell of Ballingry, Fife, Scotland off 8½ yards

Eddie Cain of Carlisle, Cumberland, England off 7½ yards

Joe Murdoch of Stonehouse, Lanarkshire, Scotland off 8 yards

Rod Tickle of Newton-Le-Willows, Lancashire, England off 6½ yards.

With the bookies and the betting public it was obvious that Rod was one of the most fancied sprinters in this prestigious event for many years.

Sadly, for Rod and Matthew Clamp, it was not to be. Giving Eddie Cain a yard start, as he was, Rod Tickle must have literally exploded from the start because he overtook the Carlisle man and had the race in his pocket until very close to the finish when Cain came back at him and with an essentially classic dip finish took the £500 prize money and the gold medal in 11.28 seconds, with Campbell in third followed by Murdoch and Edgar.

So, for Rod to actually give Eddie Cain a start and then pass him conjures up a picture for me of an exceptionally fast starter. Albeit the Carlisle man still triumphed!

In the years following Rod's appearance at Powderhall, I received a letter from Mr. Matthew Clamp in reaction to an article I had written regarding the sprinting abilities of rugby league players. He was extolling the talent of Rod Tickle and also lamenting his disappointing result in the 1967 event. He undoubtedly felt that Rod Tickle was the fastest player in the game, certainly during that period.

Mr. Clamp was still proposing that the Leigh Rugby League Club winger was one of the best sprinters he had ever come across and, had he chosen to follow athletics as a career rather than play Rugby League, he would have been amongst the best in the World.

TURNBULL Drew: (c1930 – 2012)

Leeds have had some classy wingmen, but none classier than the Scottish Borders flier. **Drew Turnbull.** In the late 1940s and early 1950s. Drew Turnbull scored over 200 tries for his club before injury cut short his career. **The Scot told me that he clocked "even time" for the 100 yards, as he said, *"in the good old days".*** He reached international level in League.

Signed as a 17 year old from Hawick R.U. Club in 1948, Drew

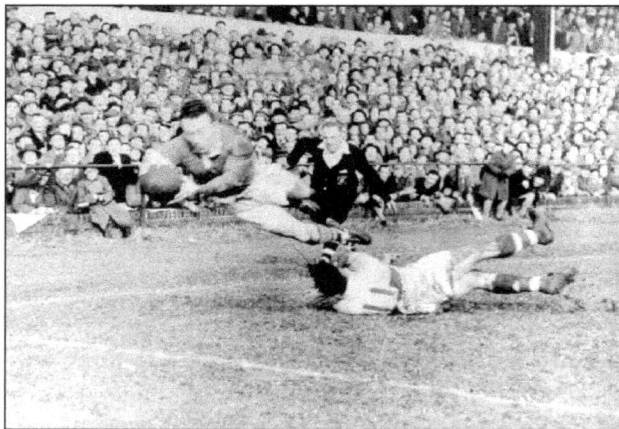

A great action shot of the Leeds flier scoring a try.
(supplied by Drew in June 1995)

won Yorkshire League Championship medals with Leeds plus selection for a Great Britain international cap and registered two tries against New Zealand in 1951. Injury curtailed his ambition to face the 1952 Australian Tourists for Great Britain. He toured Australasia in 1954 but this tour ended in tragedy for him as he had to return home early injured, after playing in two non-Test matches. Drew also represented Great Britain while at Leeds between 1952 and 1956 against France in a non-Test match. During his eight seasons with Leeds, Drew Turnbull amassed 228 tries in 230 matches. In the 1954-55 season he scored 42 tries in 26 games.

Signed by Halifax in 1956, Drew made his first appearance for the club by scoring a try at Headingley in the Halifax win against his old club.

Quoting from The Yorkshire Post of 23 June 2012 the revered Leeds club President the late Harry Jepson **stated *"Drew was a classic wingman from the Borders who knew his way to the line. He ended with a remarkable record of a try a game average over an incredible eight seasons which is up there with the very best. He could score from any distance but, close in, was like a torpedo…….. at his peak he was a nightmare for defences with his decisive runs at full pace……….he could thrill a Headingley crowd as well as any and frequently out of nothing …….."***

VAN VOLLENHOVEN Karel Thomas: (1935 – 2017)
"Voll The Flying Policeman"

This athlete, of Dutch origin and many talents, was born in Bethlehem, Orange Free State, South Africa in 1935. At the age of seventeen he joined the South African Police Force and before he was twenty years old, he gained representative honours in the fifteen a side game both with The Police and the Northern Transvaal teams.

He became a "Springbok" in 1955 when he played for his country against the British Lions:-

Filling the no.12 spot (centre) in the First Test before 90,000 at Ellis Park, Johannesburg, South Africa;

Playing wing and scoring a hat-trick of tries facing the great British Lions wing Tony O'Reilly, in the Second Test at Newlands Stadium, Cape Town, in front of 52,000;

In the Third Test, again on the wing before 45,000 at the Loftus Versfeld in Pretoria ;

By kind permission of Alex Service, Historian, Saints' Heritage Society. (2012) (www.saints.org.uk)

The Final Test, on the wing, scoring a try before 37,000 at Crusaders Ground, Port Elizabeth.

Within the Test series he also represented NE Transvaal, before 40,000 at Loftus Versfeld, scoring another try from the other centre spot number 13.

In 1956 Vollenhoven toured Australia and New Zealand with the Springboks, scoring twice against New South Wales and once against Queensland, plus a drop goal in the Second Test.

He then went on to score against Waikato and Manawatu in New Zealand. Incidentally, all his Test appearances on the wing for the Springboks were on the left side. Danie "Doc" Craven, one of South Africa's best, arguably the very best and most successful coach

of all time,who seemed to have no time quite naturally for Rugby League whatsoever, eventually recognised Tom Van Vollenhoven as a great talent taking time to point out that he was arguably the best winger in the history of the League game. This from a man who certainly was revered in South African Rugby Union.

Tom was certainly the fastest man on the Springbok side that toured Australia in 1956 and the first South African player to score three tries in a Test match in his own country..

The Flying Policeman, from being the darling of South African Rugby Union became a virtual outcast when he decided to sell his talents to Rugby League.

His name is as synonymous with St Helens as is Pilkington Glass. After some interest by Warrington in obtaining his signature as a professional and a determined effort by Wigan, Van Vollenhoven signed for Saints in late 1957 for, **as Alex Service of Saints Heritage Society reported**, £7230 – the highest fee at the time paid to a Rugby Union player or as a transfer between Rugby League clubs for any player. He then commenced a career in League that was to excite fans throughout the game, not just at Knowsley Road. Making his debut against Leeds at Knowsley Road, on October 26 1957, he scored a try in front of 23,000 fans, and went on register 45 tries in 34 appearances.

He was R.L. leading try - scorer in seasons 1958-59. 59-60 and 60-61 with 62, 54 and 59 tries respectively ; scored six tries in a game twice against Wakefield Trinity and Blackpool Borough and his career total for St Helens was 392 tries in 409 games. (That 62 tries total in 1959 broke the long standing Saints record for tries in a season held by the great Alf Ellaby.) In addition to the medals secured from the Hunslet and Wigan games mentioned below, the Springbok wing wizard took victors spoils at a further Challenge Cup Final and in five Lancashire Cups.

It is impracticable to talk about all the fantastic tries "Voll" scored, let it suffice to record that amongst Saints fans and amongst R.L. fans at large, the two best were both game breaking efforts, the first in the 1959 R.L.Championship Final at Odsal Stadium against Hunslet who had a grip on the game at 12 - 4 when "Voll" received a pass from the legendary centre Duggie Greenall with some 75 yards to go and no room whatsoever to work in. Needless to say, such circumstances as these often brought the best out of the Springbok and that day was no exception as he beat about half a dozen defenders to touch down and set Saints fair for a 44 - 22 win in which he registered a further two tries. The second occasion is without doubt the 1961 R.L.Cup Final at Wembley when leading Wigan 5 - 4, after a break by Dick Huddart, flying centre Ken Large and Voll interpassed for the remainder of the field for the flyer on the wing to finish behind the posts. Saints won the Challenge Cup 12-6.

Saints player centre, stand-off, wing, Peter Harvey recalled that - *"Voll could run in a straight line and beat people with his change of pace. In Tom's case, it was the ease with which he did everything and the ability to change pace when everyone else was running flat out.*

You could see him change gear because his head would go to one side. That was Vol stepping up from three quarter pace to overdrive. When you thought he was running flat out – and as people went to tackle him – he would accelerate away."

Voll scored a hat-trick in his last "derby" game against Wigan in his Testimonial Season, at Knowsley Road in 1968. A seven inch single called the **Vollenhoven Calypso** was released and was, in my opinion and that of many others, brilliant and, with Duggie Greenall telling a tale, very funny.

I am pleased to have purchased and retained my copy.

Alex Service further reported that :- *On May 3, 1968, for his very last match in the game of Rugby League, Voll was invited to play for a Great Britain team who were playing their final preparatory match against Halifax at Thrum Hall before going to the World Cup in Australia. His unusual finale resulted, somewhat inevitably, in a hat-trick of tries!*

Voll did play Representative Rugby League:-

For a Northern RLXIII win at Headingley in 1958 against France (19-8) Voll scored 2 tries.

For a Northern RLXIII defeat at Knowsley Road also in 1958 against France (8 - 26)

For a Rugby League XIII win at White City, Manchester in 1961 against New Zealand (22-20).

For a Rugby League XIII defeat at Parc de Princes, Paris in 1961 against France (21-20). Voll scored a try.

Karel Thomas Van Vollenhoven was poetry in motion and, in my opinion, this was arguably his greatest asset in that it all looked so easy. Opposition defences must have been fooled on countless occasions by the appearance that he wasn't moving so fast. "The Flying Policeman" as he was called by virtue of his job in his native South Africa, could long jump in excess of 24 ft. and run the 100 yards in 9.8 seconds, a time he achieved against the German athletics team. He also represented South Africa in the sprint relay event. Indeed, there are Springbok sources that credit the flyer with 9.7 seconds for the 100 yards and having cleared 25 feet in the long jump. Van Vollenhoven's athletic abilities can be better appreciated by considering the best in the World during the same period :-

In 1954 at the Vancouver, Canada, Commonwealth Games, the 100 Yards Final produced a winner clocking 9.6 seconds, the next four clocking 9.7 seconds and the last clocking 9.8 seconds ; in the Long Jump Final the winner cleared 24ft. 8¾ins. (7.54m.), the Silver medalist 24ft. 3ins. (7.39m.) and no other athlete cleared 24 feet.

At the Melbourne 1956 Olympic Games the 100 metres times, rounded up and equated to 100 yards times, showed the winner at 9.7 seconds, four at 9.9 seconds and one at 10.0 seconds.

The long jump final indicated that the first six cleared between 24ft. 1¾ins. (7.36m.) and 24ft. 8ins. (7.52m.)

Karel Thomas Van Vollenhoven is the only South African representative in the Rugby League Hall of Fame.

All aspects of playing the game of Rugby League considered, Van Vollenhoven was the greatest wingman ever and, many will argue, the fastest. Albert Rosenfeld, Brian Bevan, Lionel Cooper, Billy Boston, Bill Burgess, are a few, in my opinion, who would definitely challenge Van Vollenhoven but for all-round ability, ask any Saints fan, the flying Springbok has no peer.

Those who saw him play count themselves as privileged, for here was a truly great athlete, a legend in his playing career and I know such adjectives are used perhaps more often than they should be in modern day sport but in describing Karel Thomas Van Vollenhoven they are, at best, only adequate.

In the future, Rugby League signings may be made from a far greater variety of countries than the old favourites, Australia, New Zealand, France, South Africa, Wales & Scotland, but I earnestly believe that those of us who witnessed the all-round skills and bravery of Tom Van Vollenhoven would largely agree that he was unique amongst great athletes and his like will never be seen again.

Karel Thomas Van Vollenhoven, born Orange Free State, South Africa April 29, 1935, died Selcourt, Springs, South Africa October 21 2017.

WATKINS "Dai" David: (1942 – 2023)

"Woe betide anybody who legitimately joined Rugby League to play professional sport. When the talented and much vaunted Welsh captain David Watkins joined Salford for a King's ransom of £13,000 in 1967, it was as if he had suddenly contracted leprosy. He was friendless in the valleys".
Sean Smith – The Rugby Game – A Rugby History.

David "Dai" Watkins was a Rugby union and Rugby League international stand-off, centre, full-back of immense talent and electrifying pace.

This all-time Welsh Wizard captained the British and Irish Lions in Union, and in League, Wales and Great Britain.

In the Union scene he played club rugby for Abertillery, Ebbw Vale, Pontypool and Newport, whilst at representative level he turned out 3 times for the Barbarians in 1962, Monmouthshire, Glamorgan, Crawshays, Wales and The British and Irish Lions, making his international debut against England at 20 years of age. **With Newport he experience a win that very few can claim – against the 1963 All Blacks – the only defeat the tourists had in 36 games!**

["Crawshays" is one of the world's most iconic invitational Rugby Union sides having been in existence for nearly a century.]
[Monmouthshire County RFC is a Welsh Rugby Union club that manages an invitational team, known as "Monmouthshire" that originally played rugby at county level.]
At international level in Union Dai Watkins captained Wales on three occasions. He faced England, Ireland and France each on 5 occasions and on 4 occasions against Scotland. He also played against New Zealand and South Africa. In all at that level he had 21 games ; led The Lions in 2 Tests against the All Blacks in New Zealand in 1966.

[Incidentally veteran sports journalist Peter Jackson reminds us that Dai Watkins was the only player to have captained both the British and Irish Lions in Union and the Great Britain League side.]

The brilliant Welsh fly half, for £13,000, signed with Salford in October 1967. He was 5ft 6ins (1.68 m.) 10 stone 3lbs (64.9 kg.)

Still standing as a Salford record, he scored 147 tries, 1241 goals including 16 drop goals, before moving on to Swinton and then Cardiff. As is expected from 'The Welsh Fly Half Factory", Dai Watkins was a points machine with his double - edged sword of try scoring and goal kicking and confounded many who did not think he would succeed at League.

In the 1972–73 season - 221 goals – a total of 493 points remains the most scored by any player at the club in one season and his three tries in five minutes against Barrow in December 1972 was documented in the Guinness Book of Records'. Dai also holds the Salford record of scoring in 92 consecutive matches from 19 August 1972 to 25 April 1974.

[The great Welshman was persuaded to play for Swinton in 1979-80, turning out 20 times.]

In summary, and with some repetition from the foregoing paragraphs, this master of the game from the Welsh Fly Half Factory played Rugby League for Salford, Swinton and Cardiff with his absolutely outstanding and enduring time with Salford demonstrated by 2907 points consisting of 147 tries and 1241 goals in 407 appearances.

Included in these appearances were:

The Challenge Cup Final in 1969;

Lancashire Cup victory of 1972 plus two more appearances in the finals of 1973 and 1975;

The Players No.6 Trophy Final defeat in 1973;

League Championship victories of seasons 1973-74 and 1975-76;

BBC Floodlit Trophy win in 1975-75 season.

Dai Watkins was the Wales coach and also coached Great Britain, to the 1977 World Cup. A member of Salford's Hall of Fame and named in the club's greatest ever team, Dai Watkins played on 13 occasions for Great Britain and 22 times for Wales leading the side in the 1975 World Cup victories against France, England and New Zealand.

In 1986 New Year Honours came his way when he was awarded the MBE - Member of the Order of the British Empire-for services to Rugby League. He was inducted into the Welsh Sports Hall of Fame in 2000 and the Rugby Football League Hall of Fame in 2022.

Whether it was at stand-off, full back or centre, his pace was such that he was dangerous anywhere on the field. He, like Alex Murphy, had recognized the need for speed early in his career and had taken his sprint training very seriously indeed. Being relatively small in stature, the development of mercurial acceleration had been a valuable ally in avoiding many a battering. Repetitive work over short distances had made Watkins capable of a very quick start and acceleration that would take him clear of a defence and he used this ability to great effect.

Watkins was credited with "even time" for 100 yards and had run with some top class Welsh sprinters.

"David remains my all-time hero -brilliant, entertaining, selfless, a giant in two codes of Rugby. He had everything."
Stephen Jones Times Rugby Union journalist.

"A Potpourri of Pace"

Les DYL, a 1970s Leeds centre three-quarter, had over 20 international caps before he had reached his mid - twenties. Dyl was very fast indeed and some will tell you that he was the fastest centre ever to play the game. Who knows, they may be right!

Frank KITCHEN and Bill KINDON were Leigh wingers in the 1950s and both were examples of being in the reckoning when arguments about who was the fastest man in League raised their head. Kitchen, who was a member of the famous World Cup winning squad of 1954 and Kindon were players whom no one could disregard from the point of view of real pace. They decimated many strong defences between them with both guile and pure pace.

Rochdale Hornets and Whitehaven saw the services of the athletic physique of **Walter NICHOLSON** in the years before and after 1950 whilst, around the same period **Pat "Tex" HEWSON** was making similar efforts for the Oldham and Barrow clubs. Both were strong running wingmen in an era which perhaps surpasses all other eras in regard to the talent on the wings. (Wigan had four international wingers on their books. Many good players, throughout the game, saw a lot of "A" team football.) Both Nicholson and Hewson were regulars on the professional sprinting circuit.

Another Rochdale Hornets player of many years ago who was Powderhall class at sprinting was **Jack Williams** as indeed was former Warrington player and Salford coach **Griff Jenkins** who reports say could fly.

Graham PAUL, known as "The Cornish Express", played for Hull K.R. in the late 1950s and early 1960s. Obviously a flyer, he came from a Union stronghold and was quite a successful winger for the Humberside club whilst also an R.U. flier of no mean ability was **Joe DUCIE** who played for Whitehaven in the early 1960s. Joe was no giant and was very fast indeed.

For a period after the second world war, **George Troth** played on the wing for Bradford Northern. Although an ex - Barrow Junior League player, George was not a local that I was fortunate enough to see play. However, I did come into contact with him in the sprinting world, having trained in the squad in which George was always back marker when I was just taking up the sport of athletics. George was a successful pro sprinter and later became a dedicated and successful sprint trainer.

Joe LYDON had tremendous pace in his Widnes days, at least, and is another of those players who was so versatile, in that he could play anywhere in the backs, that often his pure sprinting ability was often overlooked, by both the spectating public and selection committees.

Hull/Hunslet/Leeds **Paul STERLING** what a character. An absolute picture of pace and scorer of one of the greatest tries ever seen in the history of the game. Started behind his own line - Leeds Rhinos versus Adelaide Rams 1997.

How many players can claim to have been selected for the World Cup in Rugby Union and Rugby League as well as the Olympics as a sprinter ? This distinctive record was that of Tongan winger **Mateaki Mafi.** However, this athlete was perhaps as good an example as any of the way in which reports of players' prowess can be misleading. Media reports suggested that he competed in the Barcelona Olympics where he clocked 10.3 seconds for 100 metres. Whilst he did compete in the games, it was not in the 100 metres but the 200 metres and his performance of 22.05 seconds being eliminated in heat 5 of the first round did not suggest a capability of anywhere near 10.3 seconds for the short sprint, more like just inside " even time". Still very fast indeed and his pace on the field of play appeared to lack little of his track speed.

In the 1950s when the French national side was a team to be more feared than they are today, they had a wingman with a world-wide reputation for sheer pace. He went by the name of **Raymond Contrastin** and scored many fine tries for France. In 18 Test matches he scored two tries against each of Australia, Great Britain and New Zealand. Inducted into the International Rugby League Hall of Fame - could he have been the fastest man to have played the game ?

Likewise, where would Wigan's Aboriginal star of the 1980s, **Johnny "Chicka" FERGUSON** have rated? Ferguson was another player, to my mind, who was perhaps underrated as regards pace. He was so elusive that often this talent was more prominent than pace. Even at the age of 36 he was one of the fastest players at Canberra Raiders.

Another Australian, whose career surrounded the years of the First World War. was a flying wing that many Aussies reckon was at least their best ever, **Harold Horder** scored over 300 tries in his career and was a very able goal - kicker too. Nicknamed "The Wonder Winger", In 1918 he won the Sprint Championship of Australian Rugby League. The New South Wales Rugby League Annual of 1928 stated "If he is not the greatest of all rugby league footballers, he is unquestionably the greatest of all wing three-quarters".

Horder's father was an athlete and Harold developed his own pace by regular sprint training. He is an NRL Hall of Fame member.

Another Kiwi / All Black / All Gold, for he toured with that 1907-08 pioneering group, was **George Smith** who eventually joined Oldham Rugby League Club for whom he played until 1916, retiring due to injury at the grand old age, for a rugby player, of 42 and having moved from the three-quarters into the forwards. During this period he scored 100 tries.

Smith was a fine all-round athlete and had in fact been the U.K. Amateur Athletic Association 120 yards High Hurdles Champion in 1902. He was one of only two Kiwis in the history of amateur athletics in England to win a sprint or hurdling A.A.A. Championship. George William Smith's track career shows that he was a phenomenal performer with many New Zealand National Titles to his name including 5 at 100 yards, 5 at 440 yards hurdles, 4 at 120 yards hurdles.

At the Australasian Championships held at The Domain, Auckland, New Zealand, 20-21 December 1901, Smith clocked 10.1 seconds in the 100 Yards Final. Such speed was obviously a major factor when he followed up with a Championship win over the 120 yards Hurdles and coupled with his endurance, saw him also take out the Championship for the 440 yards hurdles.

MACDONALD BAILEY Emmanuel:

The 1939 Amateur Athletic Association Championships saw the emergence of a young black sprinter from Trinidad who, in post - war years, would dominate British and Commonwealth sprinting as well as rank very highly at World levels.

In the days of grass and cinder tracks, Emmanuel MacDonald Bailey won the A.A.A. Sprint Championship 100 /220 yards double on no less than seven occasions and reached two Olympic Sprint Finals winning a Bronze medal in 1952, running for Great Britain. (Between 1946 and 1953 he actually held sixteen sprint titles.)

In 1953, Leigh RLFC caused a sensation in Rugby League and Athletics circles when they signed the flier, but after many weeks waiting to make his debut, which was put off because of injury, he eventually appeared on the wing in a floodlit game against Wigan!

He actually scored a try on his debut, which proved to be his one and only game. Many weeks of deliberation, due to more injuries, saw the player and the club part company, apparently amicably. Mac's times of 9.5 seconds for 100 yards and 10.2 seconds for 100 metres were certainly more than adequate for the game but at around the 32 years of age mark perhaps it was a case of an old dog not being able to learn new tricks.

Donaldson Jack:

It is said that professional athletics in Australia has its roots in the gold fields where miners used to race in handicaps for the prize of a gold nugget. The prize was called a "Gift". It is from such background that the famous Australian handicap events, such as The Stawell Gift, originate. Jack Donaldson was born in the state

of Victoria in 1886 and became one of the greatest sprinters, amateur or professional, of all time. He held several world records and his 65 yards clocking of 6.5 seconds, set in 1910 was still standing (over 100 years)well into the current century as a professional mark. Until Ken Irvine, the Kangaroo Test winger, narrowly broke Donaldson's 100 yards world record in 1963 with a 9.3 seconds clocking, the "Blue Streak" as Donaldson was nicknamed because of the colour of his running kit, had held the record for a massive 53 years!

This great athlete did much of his running in South Africa and Scotland as well as in the Manchester area of England. It was during this time that he ran off scratch in a 300 yards handicap, at The Weaste in Salford, where he officially clocked 29.95 seconds for a new World Best performance.

My father told me that Donaldson actually turned out for Salford R.L.F.C. on the wing in a trial but nothing came of the attempt. Perhaps his slight build at a little over 10 stones(63.5 kg.) in weight was too big a handicap to overcome in such a tough and demanding sport as Rugby League.

It is often said that athletes today have a more scientific approach to training than those of yesteryear. Take it from me. Donaldson's regime was such that only a full - time athlete could have attempted to follow it!

ROWE Arthur:

This sixteen stones (102 kg.) plus shot putter was Amateur Athletic Association Champion on no less than 5 occasions and regularly represented Great Britain. With an ideal physique for the game of Rugby League and undoubted strength, Rowe had actually clocked close to "even time" for 100 yards. He signed for Oldham in the early sixties with the object of becoming a star wing three quarter. I saw him play one game in that position. Oldham R.L.F.C. thought that Rowe would fare better in the pack but he did not relish the thought and the contract between the two parties was ended. Rowe went on to pursue a very successful career in the heavy events on the Highland Games professional circuit.

Players in the Modern Game of Rugby League demonstrate pace that stuns defences and the assembled spectators. There are quite a few players in both the NRL and English Rugby League who can certainly generate such pace and if trained for pure sprinting, may well succeed.

Matty Ashton of Warrington has undoubted pace as have Tee Ritson of St Helens (formerly of Barrow Raiders) and Wigan Warriors flier Jai Field plus the NRL's Josh Addo-Carr. Today's fliers are writing their own history.

Using modern metric calculations the above Ashton and Ritson for example have been recorded at **Maximum Velocity** in game situations with ball in hand and wearing full rugby gear of :-

36.41kilometres per hour equivalent to 10.1139 Metres per Second or

9.89 seconds for 100 metres (Matty Ashton).

36.06 kilometres per hour equivalent to 10.0167 Metres per Second or

9.98 seconds for 100 metres (Tee Ritson)

Of course those **Maximum Velocities** do not indicate that both those excellent and exciting wingers are Olympic standard sprinters or, if I were either of them I would be changing my sporting ambitions.

Now consider that in Usain Bolt's World Record 100 metres in 9.58 seconds he had a **Maximum Velocity** of 44.176493 kilometres per hour equivalent to 12.2712 Metres per Second or 8.15 seconds for 100 metres!

His actual World Record was circa 17% inferior to that 8.15 seconds derived by using Maximum Velocity.

Apply the same principles to the current use of Maximum Velocity in Rugby League and it becomes obvious that Maximum Velocity is not an indication of overall speed but simply represents the highest level of pace at a given instant in a particular run i.e. at a moment in time.

{I have been fortunate to be able to clock Tee Ritson in game situations i.e. in attacking runs in full gear and carrying the ball over 60 metres, 50 metres and over 40 metres with an absolute flying start of circa 20 metres Tee's times equated to 11.5 for 100 metres on grass in full gear with the ball. Not bad if you ask me and close to what one would expect by applying the principle of timing over a distance not by using Maximum Velocity which to me is misleading.}

The Difference between today's fliers and those of the eras detailed in this book:-

The Players Are Fitter – Well, one thing's for sure – they have better facilities and supposedly better physiological knowledge and backup.

Fitness, facilities and nutrition are indeed factors that have been put forward on many occasions and by many knowledgeable people as reasons why they think today's players and the game are superior products to years gone by.

I will not dwell on any of these points except to say that many of the finest athletes in history never saw a synthetic running track, a barbell or a vitamin supplement!

In my opinion, unless an athlete takes advantage of his opposition by using banned substances, a truly balanced diet will always suffice his nutrition requirements.

The best facilities in the world will not help any athlete who does not possess the true desire to be a champion.

Fitness may well be the key to all success in sport, given a certain amount of basic talent, and fitness cannot be purchased by a coach for a team or coached into an individual player.

It's down to the player's desire to be the best he can be. If he has that, he'll get fit!

The Forwards Are Faster – some would argue.

Many never play a full eighty minutes nowadays do they?

Throughout the World game there have always been many pack men who could fairly scorch the turf and the likes of Dick Huddart, Kevin Ryan, Jack Grundy, John Mantle, "Rocket" Rod Reddy, Norm Cherrington, Ron Coote, Nat Silcock Jr. and many more, of times long gone, would have no problems keeping up with the pace of the game today.

Playing Surface and Kit - There are other diversities between periods of the game, such as playing surfaces which, because of the season the game is now played in, are better for most of the time anyway.

One item of kit that I have a particular interest in is the boot! I have never seen a boot to compare with the type I and many others wore in the 1950s. A company called Fosters, from Bolton in Lancashire, produced a truly made to measure boot that was the lightest and most pliable I have ever seen. I still possess mine and, at size 12, they weigh in at less than 300 grams each. Many players of that era wore this particular brand of footwear which, in fact, was only a running shoe with an extended piece of soft leather to protect the ankle joint and studs instead of spikes. They were certainly manufactured with the aim in mind of aiding in the production of real pace for the wearer.

[Today at 313 grams the Adidas RS15 is one of the lightest boots available.]

Another example - protective kit being worn as I remember the game in the '50s was basically a somewhat restrictive shoulder pad unit.

I am not commenting on the need or otherwise for such items in any era but I am saying that, as far as pace is concerned, it is the one facet of an individual's play that is bound to suffer.

Top Dozen:-

With the amazing amount of sprinting talent that has been the pleasure of the League fan to watch throughout the decades largely covered in this work, who would place in the top ranks? Well. on the basis of what I have considered to be valid information for many years, purely on authentic times achieved by the players concerned, in bona-fide athletic competition, my **Top Dozen** would rank as follows:-

(Where 100 yards times apply, they have been converted to 100 metres equivalents.)

KEN IRVINE	AUSTRALIA	10.2 SEC.
BERWYN JONES	WAKEFIELD TRINITY	10.3 SEC.
ALF MEAKIN	BLACKPOOL BOROUGH	10.3 SEC.
MIKE MURRAY	BARROW	10.4 SEC
ROD TICKLE	LEIGH	10.4 SEC.
BRIAN BEVAN	WARRINGTON	10.5 SEC.
KEITH FIELDING	SALFORD	10.5 SEC.
MIICHAEL CLEARY	AUSTRALIA	10.6 SEC.
JOE LEVULA	ROCHDALE HORNETS	10.5 SEC.
RALPH McCARTEN	WORKINGTON TOWN	10.6 SEC.
WALLY McARTHUR	SALFORD	10.6 SEC.
PETER HENDERSON	HUDDERSFIELD	10.6 SEC.

I think that because of Kenny Irvine's standing as a World Record Holder, there would be little argument about his leading position.

Regarding the rest of the places it really would be anyone's guess and bear in mind, in my selection there's no Frank Castle, Tom Van Vollenhoven, Alan Edwards, "Toowoomba Ghost" Eric Harris, Alf Ellaby, Stan McCormick, Bill Burgess, Martin Offiah, Willie Carne, Mark Preston, Steve Renouf, or Wendell Sailor etc.

One thing absolutely certain, in my opinion, is that any "flier" currently at a professional club either in the UK or Australasia, with one or two exceptions, would be hard pushed to get within yards of those flyers such as Eric Harris, Johnny Bliss, Brian Bevan, Frank Castle, Keith Fielding, Mike Murray, Peter Henderson, Wally McArthur, Bill Burgess, Ian Moir, Ken Irvine, from the 40s/50s/60s/70s at their best. Despite today's so called improved training facilities and methods I am equally convinced that the likes of those I have named and others would be unassailable.

Ignoring the number of tries scored by individuals concerned, because so many other criteria have an effect on the total number of tries scored in a career such as injuries, length of career, success of the team, the centre three-quarter which are all factors over which the winger has little, if any, control and all of which can drastically effect the number of touchdowns he achieves, I have selected:-

A Bakers Dozen Of The Very Best

NAME	COUNTRY	PERIOD
TOM VAN VOLLENHOVEN	S.AFRICA	50s • 60s
BILLY BOSTON	WALES	50s • 60s
BRIAN BEVAN	AUSTRALIA	40s - 50s
STAN McCORMICK	ENGLAND	40s - 50s
FRANK CASTLE	ENGLAND	50s
BILL BURGESS	ENGLAND	60s
WALLY McARTHUR	AUSTRALIA	50s - 60s
MARTIN OFFIAH	ENGLAND	80s - 90s
MICK SULLIVAN	ENGLAND	50s - 60s
IKE SOUTHWARD	ENGLAND	50s - 60s
JIM LEWTHWAITE	ENGLAND	40s - 50s
TREVOR LAKE	S.AFRICA	60s
JOHN ATKINSON	ENGLAND	60s - 70s

They all had true pace, were exciting, unpredictable.

As I stated at the beginning of this work:-

Carrying the ball and in football gear on the field of play are my provisos necessary for the title "fastest".

From the point of view of match conditions,

My Top Three Of All Time Would Be:-

FRANK CASTLE

BRIAN BEVAN

TOM VAN VOLLENHOVEN

[Illustration by the late Brian Miller]

These three great athletes proved over long careers, on many occasions, just how fast they were in match conditions and carrying the ball. For my money they would have shown all of the other contenders, from any era of the game it has been my pleasure to watch in over 75 years, the way home.

Live in the present - Dream of the future - Learn from the past

I believe that the above statement is very true in most walks of life and is especially significant in sport where, more often than not, the performances of the competitors of the current time overshadow those of athletes that have gone before and are, for some reason, invariably considered the best when, in fact, in many cases they are not.

This situation is highlighted in team sports such as Rugby League, but also applies in sports where the individual competes against the individual.

My intention via this book was to draw attention to the athletic abilities of some great Rugby League/Sprinting Legends. I hope I have achieved this and that you, the reader, have enjoyed my work even if you don't agree, necessarily, with what I have said.

The Author

A Barrovian Senior Citizen, with a long and strong family connection to Athletics and Rugby of both codes going back into the 19th Century. He has followed Rugby League for over 75 years and Rugby Union for over 70 years; A sprinter up to Northern Counties Championship levels he found Wigan and St Helens Rugby League Clubs showing considerable interest in his ability; subsequently he played trials for Salford and Whitehaven, signed for the latter as an "amateur" just prior to Barrow RLFC expressing an interest. He commenced coaching from the late 1950s gaining along the way a Diploma in Physical Education (1964), Amateur Athletic Association Honorary Coaching Award (1969), then since 1972 he has the British Amateur Athletic Board accreditation as a Senior Sprints Coach; the former Health and Fitness Club owner creator of several works on athletics skills, conditioning and local history was co-architect of the Body-Tec System of Physiological Assessment used to assess the Fitness Levels of many Professional and Amateur athletes from a variety of sports including Rugby of both codes plus leading European and Commonwealth Gold Medallists. 1974 saw him receive an award from the British Olympic Association for his contribution to sport.

In the mid-1980s he was Fitness Consultant for Barrow RLFC and attended talks in Brisbane with the Rugby League scene there with a view to taking up a similar role with Brisbane Easts. He was joint founder, with the late Arthur Miller of Cockermouth, in 1975, of the ongoing very successful Cumbria Track and Field League. His knowledge of sprinting has been described as profound and his success as a coach outstanding, having coached hundreds of athletes from a wide variety of amateur and professional sports, producing winners of National Championships, Service Championships and many medallists at National levels including 44 National Finalists, 17 Service Finalists, 37 Nationally Ranked athletes, National Sprint Relay Finalists on four occasions and 10 National Schools Finalists. In the early 1980s sponsored by the President of the Northern Counties Athletics Association, Ray was invited to be interviewed for the position of National Athletics Coach. For a time, No. 3 District Secretary of The Northern Counties Athletic Association, he served on many committees and in most positions and was responsible for the organisation of major athletic competitions.

The Northern Council for Sport and Recreation made use of his knowledge and ability in production of the Regional Recreational Strategy 1981 and, also in the '80s, he was consulted on behalf of The Sports Council in regard to Coaching / Teaching / Instructing for National Vocational Qualifications. Ray served on the original Local Sports Council and was a member of the Barrow in Furness Branch of the British Olympic Association.

The Author's additional Works:

"They Could Catch Pigeons" (1996) A history of speed in the game of Rugby League.

"Dalton's Marathon Man - From Iron Ore to Gold" (2010) International professional athletics. Arthur Preston was a miner and World Class marathon runner, but he was a professional, that's why you've probably never heard of him.

"Athletics - A Local History" (2010) Covers a period of well over 100 years, generally from the 1800s up to 1988 in the Furness area of England. 3000 individuals appear in the 694 pages of this book with links to local athletics.

"Athletes From Bygone Eras Linked To The Furness District" (2021)

"More Athletes From Bygone Eras Linked To The Furness District"(2023)

"Sprinting and Relay Racing" (1976): 2nd Edition 1983. Sold worldwide.

"Speedball and The Sprinter" (June 1981) Athletics Coach Magazine

"Speedball" (1986) Fitness and Conditioning using the speedball.

"Speedball Plus" (1986) Fitness and Conditioning using the speedball.

"Sprinting - A Top Down Structure" (1986) Sprinting

"On the Wing from Stawell to Powderhall" (2012) Rugby League & Professional. Sprinting

"Early Sport in Furness" (2018)

"Coaching Sprinters & Sprint Relay + Speedball and Conditioning Sportspeople to a High Standard" (2019)

"Let's All Go Down The Strand" (2004) Local History

"The Rink Files" (2017) The History of The Dance Hall

"The Life and Times of Thomas Hollingshead R.N." (2006) Family History

"March to Your Own Drum" (2005) Family History

"Not Even For A Bus" Novel about Athletics as yet unpublished.

BIBLIOGRAPHY

www.liverpoolsthelensrugby.co.uk/page235.html

Ray French 2014

www.saints.org.uk/saints/player.php?num=15035

www.saintsrlfc.com/2011/10/31/len-killeen/

www.saints.org.uk/saints/player.php?num=15261

www.saintsrlfc.com/2017/10/21/vollenhoven-tribute-best/

Saints Heritage Society www.saints.org.uk/saints/player.php

Alexander James Murphy by Alex Service, with additional comments from Dave Dooley

www.saints.org.uk/saints/player.php?num=15898

www.facebook.com/therugbyleaguememespage/posts/alf-ellaby-1902-1993-played-392-games-for-st-helens-and-wigan-between-1926-1939-/798977874140920/

www.rugbyleagueproject.org/players/bruce-ryan/summary.html

www.www.en.wikipedia.org/wiki/Bruce_Ryan#:.

www.adb.anu.edu.au/biography/carlton-james-andrew-5505

www.en.wikipedia.org/wiki/Wally_McArthur_(rugby_league

www.nrl.com/news/2015/08/28/vale-wally-mcarthur/

www.stfrancishouse.com.au/1950s.html

St Francis House - A Home For Inland Children

www.parlinfo.aph.gov.au/parlInfo/search/display/display.w3p;query=Id%3A%22media%2Ftvprog%2F59G06%22

W.A. Coach Voices His Confidence. (1953, July 30). The West Australian (Perth, WA : 1879-1954), p. 14. Retrieved March 16, 2011, from nla.gov.au/nla.news-article49223582

Banner Now Leads Pro. Runners (1953, March 23). The Argus (Melbourne, Vic. : 1848-1954), p. 10. Retrieved March 18, 2011, from nla.gov.au/nla.news-article23234964

Rugby Player's Big Contract. (1953, November 13). The Advertiser (Adelaide, SA: 1931-1954), p. 10. Retrieved March 14, 2011, from nla.gov.au/nla.news-article48937028

Tribute To S.A, Rugby Player. (1953, November 21). The Advertiser (Adelaide, SA : 1931-1954), p. 17. Retrieved March 14, 2011, from nla.gov.au/nla.news-article48929886

"Keeping The Dream Alive" (2008) by Dave Huitson, Keith Nutter and Steve Andrews

www.rugbyleaguehub.com/who-do-you-think-you-are-mcdonald-bailey/

www.en.wikipedia.org/wiki/George_McNeill_(sprinter)

www.en.wikipedia.org/wiki/Eric_Batten

Bald, toothless chain smoker who staggered rugby league

Frank Keating

Monday 20 November 2000

The Guardian

www.theguardian.com/sport/story/0,3604,400046,00.html

The Wigan Warriors Miscellany by Ewan Phillips (The History Press 2010)

www.stawellgift.com/hall-of-fame/history

www.salfordrugbyleagueplayers.wordpress.com/category/rugby-league/

forums.rugbyleagueproject.com/index.php?topic=13080.0

www.moseleyrugby.co.uk/the-club/internationals/

Peter Smith in the *Yorkshire Evening Post* of 26th March 2020

www.sarugbyleague.co.za/

Cumberland Rugby League – 100 Greats (2002) By Robert Gate

www.rugbyleagueproject.org/players/ian-moir/summary.html

The Players Archive by David Gronow:-

www.huddersfieldrlheritage.co.uk/Archive/Written/Players/Albert_Rosenfeld.html

Hall Of Fame - Ike Southward (townrlfc.com)

www.townrlfc.com/article/557/hall-of-fame---ike-southward

www.rugbyleagueproject.org/players/dave-bolton/summary.html

www.howold.co/person/alan-hardisty/biography

www.totalrl.com/obituary-david-watkins-a-salford-and-wales-icon/

www.keighleynews.co.uk/sport/11769879.legend-terry-hollindrake-made-keighley-proud/ from Keighley news 5 Feb 2015 by ross heppenstall – sports journalist

(Neil Ormston- Rugby League Record Keepers Club).

Ken Irvine - National Rugby League Hall Of Fame | Hall of Fame (nrl.com)

www.nrl.com/hall-of-fame/players/ken-irvine/

www.therugbypaper.co.uk/features/featured-post/31229/jackson-column-berwyn-jones-paid-the-price-for-putting-family-first/

www.welshathletics.org/en/page/berwyn-jones

rugbyleague.wales/player-dai thomas

Skill, Strength, Power, Agility, are all included in the requisites of a Rugby League Player but there's ...

"No Substitute For Pace"

"High Powered and Streamlined"

Milton Keynes UK
Ingram Content Group UK Ltd.
UKHW050910020924
447772UK00013B/151